The Life Givers

The Life Givers

W. O. Thomason

3/3
BROADMAN PRESS
Nashville, Tennessee

Library of Congress Catalog Card Number: 72-90033
Dewey Decimal Classification: 248.4
Printed in the United States of America

DEDICATION

The Life Givers

is dedicated to my wife and "children"
from whom I have received life and love.

CONTENTS

The Life Givers

Introduction . . . .

I don't know where it first happened. I don't know when. I don't even know who was the first to do it.

However, I am very much aware of the fact that at sometime in my life I became conscious certain persons were having a significant effect on the way I thought, the way I felt, and the way I acted. Their influence on my life was different. It was not something that came because of my doing, but was an influence that arose out of their own power as people. Yet, this influence was one that reached to the very deepest part of my being. Their very way of living called me to my own life. It was my first awareness of a call to be. I could sense in these people that their desire for me was not the imposition of their will upon my life. It was not the control of my thoughts or actions. It was simply an invitation from them to me—an invitation to share life—to experience the hopes and dreams of all God had placed within me.

These people were people who lived in an everyday world. They were not seen by their fellowman as being uniquely endowed. Often, in fact, these individuals were looked upon as quite plain and ordinary. Nevertheless, they found a way to change the lives of other people they met.

I soon noticed that these people worked not only to call people to what they could and ought to be, but they were people who best understood when life's problems rushed in to destroy.

I became aware of the fact that evil is a reality in every man's life. Try as man may, he cannot escape forever those damages which evil brings to his life. I came to sense anew some of the deeper meanings when John wrote "For God so loved the world that He gave His only begotten Son that whosoever believeth in Him should not perish." For human life is perishable. Perishable not just in the ultimate sense of death, but in the very present sense of today.

Every mature person knows that life becomes a struggle. One cannot escape hurt, anxiety, and fear. All of these ultimately shorten man's capacity to live to his fullest potential. I have felt deep hurt in my own life. I have walked with many friends who have known the deepest hurt that humanity can experience. But I have also seen the touch of certain people as they walked among the perishing. When they touch the shoulder or the hand of a friend it brings comfort and hope. I have found there are certain people who not only know the right thing to say but when to say it—who not only know the right way to touch, but the right time to touch.

To this kind of people—those who call us to be and those who heal us when evil has struck, I have given the name Life Givers. And today, as I think back over my life, I realize that there have been scores of people who were life givers. I regret that not all who have touched my life have been life givers. For I have known many who have taken from me that which I could not spare and who have given to me that which I did not need. This is their way of life. Fortunately this is not the only kind of people among us today. But because of them I have become more convinced that humanity cannot go on forever ignoring the existence of the life givers. We must acknowledge the presence of these people. We must reward them with our appreciation of their existence.

The idea of life giving and life givers is not a new one. In the Bible the apostle Paul refers to Scripture which spoke of Jesus Christ in these terms. The Scripture says, "The first man, Adam, was created a living being, but the last Adam is the life giving spirit" (1 Corinthians 15:45). There is a difference in men. Some live their lives as a descendant of man the homo sapien species. They are mere men. Others, however, sense a capacity to be life giving spirits. And through their lifetime are forever giving that others may live.

Many people may have trouble when others claim to have the power that Jesus Christ held. They may ask, "How can that be? Can some men give life?" Again the apostle Paul spoke to this when he wrote to the Corinthians regarding his own work of life giving in their midst.

> You yourselves are the letter we have, written on our hearts, for everyone to know and read. It is clear that Christ himself wrote this letter, and sent it by us. It is written not with ink on stone tablets, but on human hearts, with the Spirit of the living God.
>
> We say this because we have confidence in God through Christ. For there is nothing in us that allows us to claim that we are capable of doing this work. The capacity we have comes from God, for it is he who made us capable of serving the new covenant, which consists not of a written law but of the Spirit. (2 Corinthians 3:2-6)

The life giving capacity is a gift to certain persons from God. Anyone who has had the experience of receiving life from another senses that this capacity is something other than the manipulation of men. What can we say then about those life givers who do not claim to be Christians and who do not live even within a Christian society? If one carefully reads the Bible through he will discover that God is no respecter of persons. He has used men of all kinds and many beliefs to bring the word of life to other men. When the disciples of Jesus reported to him that there were others in the land who were healing in his name, that is giving life to others, Jesus said "Leave them alone." It was not difficult for the Lord to realize that in a world so completely filled with evil and with the damages that evil does to humanity, that there will never be enough of his professing disciples to bring the word of life to men.

One of the earliest recognitions that I had regarding life givers is this. They do not ask by whose right or authority they act. It has been equally true that the life givers I have known care little for the credit for the service they render. These people are caught up in a way of life. They must be busy giving what other men need to live. Whether or not the person who receives acknowledges the gift with an expression of appreciation is of little consequence to the life giver. He goes on giving as long as there are men with needs.

Deliberate intervention is perhaps the most characteristic behavior of the person who is a life giver. It is peculiar but true that humanity as a whole has the capacity to stand by and watch friends and strangers alike destroy themselves. Many times I have discussed with other people what they saw happening in the life of a friend or a neighbor. They have told in gruesome detail what they saw happening even before it happened. They have described critical moments when they knew their friend or neighbor was in a life crisis. Yet, they stood by as if they were made of stone, unable to respond.

Such behavior does not characterize the life style of a life giver. He deliberately intervenes even when there is possibility of his being rejected, misunderstood, or even attacked. He senses not only the critical situation in the lives of other people, but that people depend upon others for help in critical times. The life giver knows how foolish is the idea that a person can make it on his own.

Perhaps the greatest single mistake that humanity fosters regarding itself is this idea that a man can live successfully alone. I am not speaking of man's need for fellowship with other men but to his need for others if he is to cope successfully with his own life. He cannot do so if he is bound to the ideas and the behaviors which he alone constructs. Some men try. Some men boast that they live by their own strength, that they will not depend upon others. But there is no record of a successful life where this philosophy has been applied. We readily accept the fact that children cannot mature except their parents intervene to feed them, to clothe them, and to teach them. Many live with the mistaken idea that somewhere in life a child becomes a man and in so doing no longer needs other people to support him. Because of this most life givers have found it necessary to intervene deliberately, offering their gift to a man who needs it; but often to men who have little awareness that the gift is being offered and who have even less capacity to receive.

Life giving is not just a way of acting to people who are in obvious crisis as we normally think of crisis. It is a way of offering life to a person as he matures normally. In fact, it is the person who has had continuing relationship with a competent life giver or life givers who does mature normally. Through this relationship he comes to understand himself. He comes to believe in himself. He comes to see life as something that can be truly lived to the fullest. He comes to take from other men all that they have to offer and give all he can give. He disdains no one, but learns from all.

An older friend of mine, a life giver himself, taught me about this. He was an outstanding educator who had learned from skilled professors in the great universities of America. Although a middle-aged man when I first met him, he had not stopped growing. He was still learning. When I observed his pattern of continuing growth, I was intrigued because he learned something almost every day of his life. But the most amazing fact was not that he learned daily but from whom he learned. I heard him say once "Anyone can teach me—even the man who picks up my garbage." This successful person had learned what all of us need to know. Living is a matter of learning and learning is a way of life. And along the learning way of life there are life givers.

The writing of this book is for a two-fold purpose.

It is to establish that certain people have the capacity to be life givers. And it is to point out that people are perishing for the lack of life givers. It is my hope to awaken within readers the awareness that they have unrealized capacities to give life to perish-

ing humanity. It is to challenge those who now practice this gift
to do so more effectively. It is to call forth in life givers a new
quality of courage. This courage must consist of the capacity to
deliberately intervene in the lives of men and women whose lives
will be destroyed if no person enters in.

ONE

Our Perishing World

As I crossed the enormous lobby of a large Dallas hotel, the woman walked through the mechanically operated doorway. As we noticed each other she increased her pace, heels clicking lightly on the marble floor. A smile flooded her face lending it a brightness like the Texas sunlight coming through the door behind her. In a moment she had stopped before me, reached up, and hugged my neck. The warmth of her embrace quickly caused the memory of our first meeting to enter my consciousness.

This attractive young woman had come to see me some four years earlier as the result of an invitation through her husband. She arrived at my home looking quite different from this day. Her clothing seemed to have been thrown on. Little care had been given to it for weeks. The suit collar was turned inside her jacket. The hem line of her skirt slanted oddly with the floor. Her face was creased, distraught, and clouded. There was not a trace of cosmetics. Anxious eyes looked from under eyelids puffed from recent crying. A timid hand reached out to mine.

Our first meeting together was a long, emotionally packed hour. I listened while she described confused feelings and ideas. She despised her life. She longed for death. She felt she was the worst person, the worst wife, and the worst mother in all the world. Twice she had been in a state operated mental institution; once in a psychiatric ward of a private hospital. The day a friend of mine accidentally met her husband in a downtown store, he was making preparations for her to return for the third time to the state hospital. The husband expressed the hopelessness of their situation. He was afraid his wife would never be well again. His depression made this friend of mine intervene with the suggestion that he bring his wife to see me.

The husband called that day. "Would you see my wife?" he asked after he had told me of the depressing outlook for their home and family. Despite my training for the field of counseling, the anticipation of failure pressed into my consciousness. Could I deliberately intervene in the life of a person whose behavior pattern seemed to doom her to tragedy? In those moments of deep thought I remembered my God-given commitment to all mankind. My responsibility to act, not my likelihood of failure, gave me courage to say yes. Soon we were engaged in a life giving adventure. This young woman took increasing responsibility for sorting out her ideas and feelings, understanding their meaning, and changing her way of thinking, feeling, and doing.

Now she stood before me talking excitedly about her life. It was a life of happiness and expectation rather than one of depression and destruction. This incident is not a rare one. People with problems are as common as the air we breathe. Each day you and I pass people who have problems more serious than that described above. Scores of others have problems that they will not be able to solve by themselves. The uncommon thing is that we pay so little attention to people and their cries for help in solving their problems.

How are we able to overlook the needs of people in going to and fro in our community or as we work all day long with fellow workers, or as we spend the evening and night with our families? Why is it so difficult for us to respond to cries of people who need help? I am afraid we're taking people and their problems too lightly, either because we are too preoccupied with our own needs or because we do not sense that these people are truly perishing.

We have not yet been able to focus our attention adequately on the fact that personality is a perishable thing. We somehow think that the personality is as stable and unchangeable as their physical bodies. We are inclined to believe that changes in personality, or damage to personality, is as slow in coming as gray hair to a young man or flabby muscles to a strong body. We lack the capacity for insight into what is taking place inside the people around us. This is strange since what is happening to them is on occasions also happening to us. We have even learned to treat ourselves harshly, ignoring our own needs. We have lost the ability to express consciously that our own being is hurting or perishing.

We are acquainted with the biological fact that millions of cells in our bodies are dying on a regular cycle. We know that in due time all of the body is replaced by new cells. We are unconscious of this function and care little that it is happening or when it is happening. We trust our subconscious minds to take care of this function. We're often equally as unconcerned and unconscious of the daily erosion in our personality, or in the personality of other people. It is not difficult to sense that people are having problems once we allow ourselves to see humanity as a group of perishing people. In the normal course of a week we encounter numerous people who clearly signal to everyone around them that they are coming apart on the inside. Sometimes this coming apart is in a very narrow area of their life. Other times it is at the very heart of all of their life.

The remainder of this chapter seeks to illustrate how often in a week we encounter people needing help. The eight incidents described represent one third of the people who discussed problems with me during one week. The week was an ordinary one in my life. Any reader of this book could have had similar experiences.

The illustrations may prove to be uninteresting since I do not tell whether the people successfully resolve their problems. Our need to have all conflicts resolved successfully, to have Cinderella endings, sometimes prevents us from seeing life as it is. My hope is that you can see in these illustrations people you passed last week—or last month. Or perhaps you will be challenged to listen more carefully for the requests for help that come in ordinary conversation in the ordinary places that people meet.

The names used in these and most other personal illustrations in this book are fictitious but the incidents are as real as life itself.

Jack is a college student, attending a large Southern university. He is uncertain as to what he will do with his life. He is taking courses in which he spends many hours of time studying, storing up mental skills which he can use in his adult life. Since he is uncertain what his vocation will be, he prepares himself with little idea of how he will use his skills and even a question of whether he will ever use the skills. Interestingly enough this university provides guidance and help but Jack, like many other students, has not spent even one hour making use of these resources. He is struggling alone on the problem of the occupation he should follow.

Jane is a person who gets over involved with people. She will let them take more of her time and control her life beyond that which is healthy for her. Her need to be depended upon comes out of her early life. How it developed and what need it met are unclear to Jane. She only knows that after awhile in some relationships she needs help to get through.

Joe is a fellow who has difficulty working successfully. He cannot stay at the job. He finds that concentration and attention on the hard parts of his work are impossible. More and more he has found that it is impossible to work a full day. He finds himself sitting and looking at the work that should be done. He knows that this behavior will soon cause him to lose his job. He has a family to support. Now he is faced not only with his inability to concentrate but with a high level of anxiety for fear of what will happen.

Ruby is a middle-aged woman. She is a very affectionate person needing not only to give affection but to receive it. She married what she thought was an affectionate person. But soon learned affection was not given freely by her husband. Her husband does love. He does need affection. He does give some affection, but not enough. Ruby has reached the stage where she has a poverty of affection.

Tom has a wife whose illness may be terminal. He finds it difficult to let her die. Inside he feels constrained to work at the job of making his wife live whether she wants to or not. He is filled with guilt feelings and anxiety. He has a real problem in allowing his wife's physical life to perish without letting his own personality perish.

James, in his mid thirties, is a successful professional with graduate degrees. He is well settled in his engineering profession. He denied himself deep personal relationships with anyone in order that he might achieve this goal. He came out of a family situation where concepts of achievement and financial capacities were limited. He determined early to go beyond his parents' achievement. His struggle caused him to deny himself many of the experiences normal to human life. He would not allow himself to think of marriage nor to develop a relationship that could lead to marriage. Now he has achieved his professional goal. He is a success. His need for companionship or his need for one significant life relationship on the level which marriage brings has become primary. He needs to find a person with whom he can share on a deep personal level.

Al learned this week he has a disease which will limit him physically perhaps even bringing a premature death. In the past two or three months, he experienced some symptoms which he could not understand. Now the facts are in. He is facing these facts and their meaning to him in terms of his own personal struggle; the meanings to him in terms of the effects of his circumstances upon his wife, his children, and his business. His whole life must be looked at anew. The question is how one can completely rearrange a life after having worked so many years to establish patterns of acting and relating? How can one cope with this problem when energy itself will be less than he has ever had in his life?

Marilyn wants to be. She's a capable young person. She is well trained in both mental and professional activities. But she finds that too many people want to direct her life: Parents who still want to tell her how she should do something and where she should do it. Colleagues who want to remove the last iota of ineffectiveness from her behavior. Friends who too often pick at small unimportant habits rather than calling her to more important possibilities. She finds herself wanting to fight from the inside with people who are important to her on the outside. How will she be able to become the person that she is capable of becoming and yet not lose the significant relationships in her life?

Janet's letter came on Thursday. She was extremely anxious. She had told me before of the concern she had for her life. She no longer felt the exhilaration of earlier years. Her children were grown and had left home. Her life was now built around pleasing her husband. But this was not enough. Her search to find herself was not as successful as she had hoped. She felt depression as she contemplated long years without meaning. Her letter poured out these feelings and these ideas to me. She did not ask that someone assume her responsibility to solve her problem. But she did write how she could use help in her search for a purpose.

J. N.'s call came long distance on Friday night. His company was reorganizing. He had had trouble with the top management for some time. Although he recognized that some of the difficulties were of his own making he didn't feel it was all his fault. Some were due to an incompetency on the part of the management in his company. He was angry but he was also afraid. What would he do? What could he do? Would a middle-aged man be able to re-establish himself at this time. What about his self respect? What of his family's self-esteem?

Some of these people have successfully solved their problems. Others have not. What will become of them? Our perishing world cannot tolerate a passive response by those who have been sent to give it life. I am thinking of people whom I have seen during the past month whose lives were in shambles because no one had adequately responded to their needs. Everyone had assumed they wanted their life the way it was. People felt that they didn't care to have anything better. So these people were left alone. And being left alone their solutions to real life problems were those constructed out of their own blindness.

Donald has two delinquent sons. One is now at the age that he is beyond his father's legal control. The younger son is still Donald's responsibility. The problems of this family have existed for many years. The father has irrationally rushed from one social agency to another seeking help in coping with his sons. Friends of his watched the situation and on occasions made observations. Most of these comments have regarded the behavior of the sons. The people have said that this behavior just can't be accepted and that he as father must do something about it.

Few of those who have observed the situation looked deeply enough into the family situation to really know what would have helped. Yet, information about how the family lived was available to them for not only could all the neighbors see what was going on, but Donald himself freely described everything that took place. Donald's behavior was inadequate and destructive. Unfortunately, some of the people who thought they knew the real problem refused to get involved. They stood by passively watching Donald's inadequate behavior push his children further toward the brink of destruction. Even Donald's wife knew what the problem was, but she was unable to pay the price to effect a change in his behavior. It was a fairly simple thing, but by being left alone it is now a problem of vast proportions. There is a good possibility that the lives of both sons will never be normal. Society will pay a heavy price many times over because some people chose to do nothing.

Mary and Bob are getting a divorce. They've been married for over twenty years. Both are wonderful, likable people, with many friends. Their early years of marriage were happy years. They did many things together and were helpful in making life happy for their children and for many of their friends. Now their children are almost grown, fairly well adjusted, and apparently on the road to becoming a success. But several years ago Mary and Bob began a behavior which led to this divorce. I can recall close friends of theirs making observations that Mary and Bob should be careful. Later these observations grew to express the concern that the problem was getting serious. Now the results of the problem are leading to the destruction of a marriage and a home. Why did these friends who made observations to everyone but Mary and Bob not act for this couple? How could they see what was going on and not offer help? Do they not believe that unhealthy behavior will ultimately bear the fruit of death?

People in the perishing world think strangely. They think that human beings live life in isolation. Somehow they have concluded that people who are identified by a family name, a business name, a church name, or a race name live separately and that somehow within this isolated group an individual lives out all his life and finds answers to all of his problems. This is not so, nor will it ever be so.

Man must come to the belief that the life of one man is bound to the lives of all other men. I am aware that this becomes a difficult premise to accept when we try to make the life of an American relate to that of an isolated Chinese. But only as the American perceives his relationship to all men to be tied up with his own success will he respond adequately to the men who live in his neighborhood. The Smiths, the Johns, the Scotts, and the Browns are all together in the valley of the shadow of death. It is to one another's cries for help that they listen. They live in the overflow of anxiety and fear which exists in one family or the other.

In this decade when there is massive concern for the ecology of our natural resources, it is equally time for a massive concern for the ecology of human personality. When we are giving our attention to people who are polluting our world with physical garbage we should also be concerned with those who drag the emotional garbage and debris from wrecked human life along our highways. During years when we are spending more money and time to reduce the poverty of physical possessions, we need to give more attention to the grave poverty of affection which is hidden away in the lives of our friends and fellowmen.

TWO

Deliberate Intervention

I grew up in a southern city. Our home was located on the side of a hill. The street was well paved with strong gutters on either side. One of the happy play experiences of childhood was to rush out of my home after a heavy shower and play in the water as it tumbled down the hillside. It was a thrill to roll my trousers up to the knee and to wade uphill feeling the water rushing around my ankles. Near my home there was a outlet into which the rain water could go. I can recall becoming intrigued with the way water rushed and swirled into this manhole. In its power, trash and debris would be carried along by the waters. One particularly interesting and exciting activity was to dam up the water. This was more interesting when the dam could be built in such a fashion that debris could be caught behind the dam with the water eddying out into the street and working its way back to the manhole. A sort of elation at being able to "save" the trash through this activity which I performed filled me. I suppose this was my first sensing of the great capacity which God created in man. It is the capacity to intervene.

I previously called attention to the great need for us to intervene deliberately into the predicaments of our fellowman; how by offering help deliberately a person may be saved from many of life's predicaments. This experience of my childhood awakened in my thinking this possibility which is uniquely ours as human beings. I have marvelled and admired the activity of deliberate intervention on the part of man throughout all history. The little dam which I built in the gutter near my home is child's play when placed against the Boulder Dam and other great construction efforts by engineers. Through their efforts the course of the great streams of our world have been changed. The power of these streams have been controlled for the good of the people in the nearby area and for long distances away. Valleys have been made green and productive. The power that comes from these great dams sustains the industry and life of great cities. The capacity to store up water in order to supply equal amounts to a vastly growing population has resulted. Few of us see these as results of the deliberate intervention of men into the natural ways of nature.

The Declaration of Independence is a great act of deliberate intervention. Men who no longer cared for governmental rule as it was known and practiced during the 17th and 18th centuries banded together in the Colonies of an undeveloped North America and spoke their intentions. They built a dam across the pathway of undemocratic government. And out of this deliberate intervention the United States has grown into a powerful nation.

Taking medicine is deliberate intervention in an occurrence of sickness. Taking an aspirin is nothing more than deliberately intervening to stop the pain and ache that we feel in our body. Through the use of medicine we deliberately intervene in biological or chemical processes of our body. Thus we alter what is taking place. Therefore, the makers of medicine are themselves deliberately intervening in the physical processes of our bodies.

Deliberate intervention occurred when the United States joined allies in defeating the course which Hitler had in mind for his German nation.

Deliberate intervention is not just turning aside evil or destruction by the placing of an obstacle or a deterrent. It is also the deliberate intervention for positively aiding a person to become what he can be. Deliberate intervention was my pastor showing me the kind of life that was possible if I lived it in accordance with the teachings and gifts of Jesus Christ. It was a high school teacher, who saw me goofing off instead of performing in a superior fashion, getting angry enough to upset me with myself. It was a mother who, many times when I didn't want her to do so, saying in private, "Bill, I'm proud of you." It was a respected friend saying to me "Do you know that you have some special abilities in helping people who are in need. What are you going to do about them?"

These intentional interventions, like many others in my life, have made it more abundant. In fact, the timeliness with which these people acted has caused me to have a fuller life much longer than if they had been hesitant, passive, or slow to intervene.

Think of the catastrophes and failures that humanity has known either because no one deliberately intervened or because the intervention was on an untimely schedule. Moses would not deliberately intervene between the two groups of spies who had searched out the promised land. As a result of his unwillingness to intervene in behalf of the believing Joshua and Caleb, the Israelites spent an unnecessary forty years in the deserted lands between Egypt and Palestine. Because no one intervened, the position of women in the society and family was for centuries that of property, the possession of a man to be disposed of at his will. Mentally ill people were for centuries locked and chained in prisons and dungeons because no one would deliberately intervene in their behalf. Black people in our nation lived for a century or more as second-class citizens because no one in the white race was willing to pay the price of deliberate intervention. More than thirty people stood passively by and watched the life stabbed out of a young woman on the staircase of a New York City building.

But the real tragedies are not these which are well known to those of us in the Western World. The great tragedy is the millions of single tragedies occurring daily in our midst. Fragments of these dramas we see. Sufficient signals are flashed to us to alert our senses and our feelings. Yet we stand by and fail to intervene.

What is deliberate intervention? Deliberate intervention has three aspects to it. It is assuming responsibility to offer help to our fellow-man in his predicament. It includes making a specific decision in terms of a specific person's need. It is acting in a timely and insightful manner according to this person's need.

Being responsible is a very difficult task. It has been quite interesting through the years to observe that the people whom I have counseled are seldom adequately responsible for themselves. It is amazing to me the kind of predicaments into which people will allow themselves to get. Even the simple matter of providing adequate physical care or rest is an area in which scores of people act irresponsibly toward themselves.

What is true about people and themselves is even more true when it comes to being responsible to offer help to others—whether they are friends or strangers. The weight of responsibility is too heavy for most of us. For some reason we have the mistaken idea that to offer help to another person, even when freely taken, makes us totally responsible for the results whether they are a success or a failure. Some day we must come to see that offered help does not itself make us responsible for the life of another person. Deliberate intervention is not concerned with the results of the intervention but only the offering of help. In all the years I have been offering help to people I have encountered only a handful who sought afterwards to hold me responsible for a situation that became worse. The fear of blame, however, does cause many to shirk a responsibility that is evident within the very nature of humanity.

The most dramatic act of deliberate intervention was that of God himself in Jesus Christ. The Scriptures say that in the fullness of time God sent his Son. The Scriptures teach us that from the foundation of the world God intended to intervene with Jesus Christ. When we consider the situation that exists in the world of people who have not found out how to live with themselves or their fellowman and the hopeless possibility of their ever learning to do so, we are confronted with the kind of problem that God looked upon. He sensed man's need. He saw man's need to be loved while he was still evil, man's need to be allowed to find himself, man's need to be shown a better way of acting than the one he learned from his human father. God saw men who had little hope of learning how to live differently since others were unable to model for him a better way of life. It was to this kind of world and these kinds of people that Jesus came. Herein we find the real meaning of the words, "For God so loved the world that he sent his only begotten son," or the words that "God commended his love toward us in that while we were yet sinners Christ died for us." These were acts of deliberate intervention.

We miss a great deal of the message of God if we see in the coming, death, and resurrection of Christ only the salvation experience. There is more. The message for us to be sent even as God sent Jesus Christ is the commission to engage in deliberate intervention. Also, we must look beyond the acts of crucifixion and resurrection when we think of the life that Jesus Christ came to give. For he did not wait for his death and resurrection to give life. He, with the woman beside the well in Samaria, deliberately intervened in a household and community problem which he could have been told was none of his business. He stepped forward when the Jews asked him to respond to their intent to stone a prostitute and deliberately intervened in her behalf. He could have been called a liberal and himself stoned in light of his interpretation of the Scripture and his life giving response to this woman. No better words describe the activity of God toward the world through Jesus Christ than Deliberate Intervenor. The world has never been the same. It will never be the same because of his acts. It is now a vastly better world and a world with a vastly greater possibility than it was before this intervention.

Decision-making is a rare activity. I'm sure there are those who will read this statement and disagree. But when we observe human beings all day long, day after day, we soon discover that they really make very few decisions. Human life, especially by the time of adulthood, is too much an activity of acting from habit. Habitual behavior does not require conscious thought or decision making. Thus most of what we do is done without the decision-making process. As a rule, this is not bad for it would consume vast amounts of our intellectual capacity, our energy, and our time if we were still engaged in making decisions in a logical step by step analysis of every act we take during a day. However, because we have the benefit of making habits out of certain behaviors, we should not make life nothing more than a set of patterned behaviors.

If we are going to make a real difference in our world and particularly in the lives of people who need our help, we must become conscious decision makers. We must learn to observe the way things really are. We must learn that decision-making is the conscious conclusion that it's time to do something. In deliberate intervention we must develop the capacity to respond consciously. We must think in order that we might decide. And we must decide in order that we might act. In decision-making we are dealing with the part of human personality that allows us to move from a thinking position to an acting position. Decision-making has to do with our will to act or our unwillingness to act. In deliberate intervention decision-making plays a major part.

The essence of deliberate intervention, however, is the offer of timely and insightful help. This is not a skill that everyone has. It is, however, a skill that most people could have if they were willing to devote time to its development. Insightful action is that kind which grows out of understanding what the situation really is. Timeliness is offering this insight to a person when he can most effectively accept and use it.

Recently I was talking with all five members of a family. We were discussing the way the father acted in certain situations. The other members of the family felt the father was a most suspicious person. They concluded that he was hard to fool, self-opinionated, and therefore a difficult person with which to live. As I observed his behavior I saw something different. He was a man with exceptional capacities to think through problems and to analyze rapidly. He had established the habit of analyzing so well that he could analyze any situation in a few moments. On the other hand he took things very seriously. In fact, he took many things too seriously. Therefore, when he began to apply his highly analytical thinking capacity to a situation that the rest of the family took less seriously, he appeared to be suspicious. They saw him as one who was scrutinizing: turning over and looking under every rock to find evidence with which to prosecute them. He had little awareness that his intense seriousness with his exceptional capacity to analyze was being misunderstood and thus creating a hurtful atmosphere. On the other hand, his family looked only at the surface and were reaching wrong conclusions. Therefore they were relating wrongly to this man. At a proper time it was possible to offer an insight to the family to help them to see that their misjudgment of this particular behavior was creating part of the problem which the family had gathered together to discuss.

Offering the insight and offering it at what appeared to be a timely moment did not make it mandatory to the family to use this insight. Nor did it make me responsible for their proper and effective use of it. However, it could be the bridge to restored relationships and to life giving results. Acting in a timely and insightful fashion is something that we have not been formally taught to do in our educational experiences. It is not something that we have universally learned in our families. Therefore, we can expect and can observe that most people relate to other people not on the basis of what they see going on, but on the basis of what *they hear and feel* is taking place.

Why don't people get involved? Perhaps it is better to speak to the question of why people do get involved. Acting deliberately or intentionally is the result of something existing in the person rather than the result of being kept from acting. Intervention is the result of having *life* within one's self, having *insight* into the situations of the hurt and helpless, and having *courage* to risk failure or rejection. Life. Insight. Courage. These are the ingredients which cause one to intervene deliberately.

One cannot give what one does not have. Therefore, if one is to deliberately offer life to another, he must have life within himself. One would think this should qualify everyone since we have all lived and the accumulation of this experience is itself life. However, life that we offer to another in time of need is not just the accumulation of days or years of experiences. It is the truth which we have gathered from these experiences. Some people have managed to live long lives and really never develop any sense of meaning from all that they have done. You have perhaps seen people who go through their life acting in a manner that creates problems and hurt for people around them. They do the same thing year in and year out, decade after decade. You say to yourself, "Won't they ever learn?" The answer, of course, is "No, unless someone deliberately intervenes, they never will learn." The truth that some men are able to gather from their life experiences becomes to them a source of life. This becomes a source of life not only for themselves but a source of life for others around them. People who act intentionally to offer the truth they have found are those who have become aware of this wealth of truth within them.

We often see these people as those who are ready to give advice. It is true that these people are ready to offer help in the form of advice, but we must not mistake every advice giver as a life giver who is able to intervene deliberately. Many people who are supposedly offering advice are offering an artificial truth. All men who talk do not say something with meaning. And many people who listen, or who say they are listening, are not able to distinguish between the word giver and the source of truth.

The life giver is one who deliberately intervenes with insights into the situation to which he is speaking. Although many of us share common experiences, life has dealt with each of us in a unique way. When we get a group of people together each person in that group has had a number of experiences which are his and his alone. Therefore, the possibility to understand life is to some degree dependent upon the breadth and type of experiences that one has had. How these experiences were lived is another factor in intervention. When some people describe their experiences they show they know what took place as far as seeing with the eyes is concerned, but they lack little ability to see into the real situation. They overlook feelings that were present. They overlook subtle communications which took place. They fail to understand the meanings of complex relationships. This is another way to say they lack insight into what was happening.

Deliberate intervention calls for a person to be able to look into a situation and separate those observable activities which one can see taking place from the feelings that are present. Sometimes feelings are seen only by the color or reflection of the eyes, the color of their cheek or the movement of a hand. This person must be able to analyze the relationship between an outside observable act and something that happened five or ten years earlier in the life of another person.

One might say, "How can one ever develop the ability to see into situations and draw conclusions or insights from these situations". It depends upon how we have been trained. On a number of occasions I have received real enjoyment in observing other people begin to see into situations or see into the actions or words of another person. They always get excited and interested as they realize that what they are seeing has always been there for them to see. But we say, "How can we relate what one is doing or saying today to something that he has done or said five or ten years earlier when we've never known the person?" Sometimes I wish that human behavior and human beings were so different that none were at all alike. It would certainly make for an exciting world. But the truth is this isn't so. People keep on acting like people, and the way we feel things today, say things today, act things today is not completely different from the way men have done through the ages. Therefore, the individual who is trained is able to recognize that a certain way of acting must grow out of some experience of earlier life which is very similar to that of other people that we have known. Thus just being one who has lived insightfully awhile develops a reservoir of information which can be offered as help to the next individual we see in need.

After all, man has been having problems since he was first created. He has been hurting, he has been lonely, and he has been greedy. He has been good and bad. He has been angry. He has been fearful. He has been all the things that we are now. Because man has already been so much of what we are today, we should be able to understand what's going on when we see ourselves, our friends, and even strangers hurting, lonely, angry, or good and bad.

Courage is a quality that we really know little about. We talk about it. We speak of a person doing a courageous act. Or we more likely say, "I wish I could do that," meaning I wish I had the courage to do what someone else has done or is doing. A dictionary definition says that courage is the quality of mind that enables one to meet danger without fear. Another definition of courage is fearlessness. I do not agree with this definition because I believe that many people who are courageous are at the very time of their act of courage aware of a goodly amount of fear within them. Courage is the capacity to will to act even when there is evident danger. In other words, to get from a position of not acting to that of acting requires that one will to do so. The capacity to discipline or control ourselves is at the very root of our ability to will to do something where there is eminent danger to ourselves.

Each time I have begun a new walk through the valley of the shadow of death, people have seen my plight. They have cried and hurt for me. Little did they know that in the Valley of Death there is a mission. For in the valley there are persons who are afraid of the shadows—the variable lights. They fear the nearness of their own death. They do not know the experience of resurrection. These people grope and wander through the valley. Those of us who have experienced again and again our own resurrection from death, *fearing no evil*, can walk boldly and straightway through these valleys; giving insight and hope to those along the way.

We must discipline ourselves to live with fear that is crying out to be heard if we are to develop courage to act deliberately. We must come to deal with fear that blocks us from action.

I have found that fear of two things accounts for most people not intervening deliberately into situations where their help could be used. These are the fear of failure and the fear of rejection. Both of these will be discussed more in detail later. At the moment, I would simply pose the question to the reader, "Why do we need to succeed or to be accepted so badly that when we think about failing or being rejected we relinquish responsibility to our fellowman and assume a passive stance? Who has taught us to be afraid? Who has said that success and acceptance is more important than life giving? It is my conclusion that this is a myth of the world. It is a conclusion that has come to us from the creature side of our being. The fear of failure or rejection is an instinctive response to our situations. It is instinctive in the sense that we find it in the entire species. Somehow we must bring this behavior to our consciousness and evaluate it. We must look at the values to be gained by giving away this fear. We must learn to respond to life not in an instinctive fashion but in a thoughtful, logical manner, thus becoming free to offer help. We must become free to act when there is eminent danger of failure or rejection.

I have a friend who is still in his thirties. Very early in life he began to be responsible for himself. His home situation was such that if he were to experience certain things in life, it would be up to him to provide the finances and the direction for this. He soon began to engage in varying types of activities and became responsible for having an educational experience at several universities. In addition, he engaged in community activities. Before twenty-one he was making a contribution to the civic affairs of his community. He was active in his church. While still a teen-ager he taught in his church school and was a leader in youth groups. By the time he had graduated from university, he was offered the opportunity to remain on the faculty. But was given other offers in business. When I first met him some time ago he was asking a question about something that had happened. "What does this behavior of mine mean?" This intrigued me and as I sought to understand this young person I came to observe that this was a continuing question with him. I also observed how he was sought after by others not only his age but much older in years. He had something they wanted. It became very clear to me that within him there was a source of life. Already he had collected experience in a form of truth that could be offered to others. Not yet old in age, this individual sensed that he was being called to the role of intervening deliberately in the lives of people who were his friends and to many who were strangers.

I know a man who is intelligent and successful. Until a few years ago he took everything the way he saw it with his eyes. Recently, I began to notice a change in him. He began to call to my attention what was happening in other people—what was really taking place. Things of which the people were not aware and things which he had not seen before. He observed to me that one of his employees was trying to use him. He commented that this was not the first time but was something that had gone on for a number of years. Now he realized that allowing this person to manipulate him was not only unfair to himself and to others within the work situation, but it was also unfair to the individual who was doing it. He became interested in how this individual had developed this capacity to manipulate. When last talking with my friend he told me how he planned to offer this insight to this fellow worker. He was seeking to determine the proper time to make known what he had learned.

The other night I saw a magnificent thing. My wife is an invalid. The woman who lives in our home and cares for her had just experienced a tragedy in her family. It was the fourth accidental or tragic death to one of the members of her family in three years. Irma, who has worked for us only a matter of weeks, suffers deeply in her mourning and remorse. She is not very talkative. I have had little experience with remorse. I have difficulty in helping people who suffer from remorse. Sometimes Irma can go all day without saying anything about her feelings. She was in deep sorrow over this recent loss and was not responding to my efforts to share this sorrow. A friend of mine visiting in the home was aware of this sorrow and knew of my difficulty in speaking to this hurt. An eminently successful woman, she is a person most people would wrongly assume cared little for people like our home helper. While I was busy in another part of the house, she slipped into the room where Irma sat and began to talk to her. She told Irma of sorrows she had known, spoke about what the Bible and Christ meant to her. Our home helper, a very religious person, responded. She got newspaper clippings and pictures to show of her family. She talked about how prayer is almost inadequate for her at these times in life. She spoke of the problems that her family was having due to these tragedies. My friend listened and offered comfort and finally reaching over took the hand of my home helper and suggested that she pray. That night I saw a smile on two faces, one that under the circumstances has real difficulty smiling. But I also saw what courage that does not fear failure or rejection can accomplish.

What we need in order to practice deliberate intervention is what one man has called "a passion for possibility." I wish that we could awaken in all men the feeling that to try is itself to succeed. If we could exchange some of our passion for rightness and success for a passion for possibility, we would be on our way to bringing relief to a weary, hurting, and crying world. If we could feel strongly the passion for possibility, we could call people from little things they are doing in life to the great tasks of life. We could challenge people who will play games all their life to use these same talents and abilities to make great cities out of deserts, great temples out of barren churches, great educational institutions out of dirty brown school houses. They could make great havens of love out of mansions, modern apartments or ghetto houses. Deliberate intervention is the doorway to making possibilities into realities.

THREE

The Life Giving Spirit

The idea of life giving is not a new one. In fact, today it is probably receiving the most attention in the history of man. Only recently in *Reader's Digest* I read an article entitled "Invitation to Live" which contains certain ideas on life giving. The book, *The Transparent Self* by Sidney Jourard, like many books today, gives very insightful thoughts on the idea of life giving. But the very best concept of life giving and challenge to life giving is found in the teachings of Jesus Christ. This is as Christians would expect. It is interesting to study the sayings of Jesus from the standpoint of the concept of life giving. In this chapter I would like to present certain of the teachings or sayings of Jesus and discuss them in light of their meaning to life giving.

In the Introduction I referred to the Scripture in Corinthians which says "The first man, Adam, was created a living being, but the last Adam is the life giving spirit" (1 Corinthians 15:45). I'm glad that the writer of this Scripture chose to say it in just this fashion and use just these words. For this is the real difference between Jesus Christ and his kind and the people who live their lives completely like Adam. I like to think of this Scripture in connection with another one found in Corinthians which says, "When anyone is joined to Christ he is a new being: The old is gone, the new has come." In the King James version "new being" is translated as "new creature." I believe that it would not destroy the meaning of these Scriptures to suggest that any man who is truly joined in Christ is a creature of a brand new species. This species is one having the capacity to be life givers. Such a viewpoint is consistent with the teachings of Jesus found throughout the New Testament.

Consider what Jesus says as recorded in John 10:10. "I am come that they might have life and have it more abundantly." In this promise which Jesus makes he claims that through his coming humanity will come to have life and that the nature of this life will be characterized by abundance or affluency. I feel that this is particularly important. One of the strange things I have discovered in my life with people is the surprise people have when they prosper either in their mental, emotional, or physical life. It appears to them that something is strange and different. In fact, in recent decades I have been struck with the little capacity that we Americans have to live with prosperity. We better understand how to live in poverty. Isn't this the way it is with most human life when you consider the way it's lived in most of the nations of the world? Humanity lives in poverty and degradation. That's the way we live when we live according to the human way of doing things. Not so, however, when we live in freedom and in truth. For this is the life that is prosperous. Yes, it is prosperous even when those who enjoy it are beset on all sides with death and destruction. Sometimes that of their own family—even at times that of themselves.

Jesus spoke to life giving when he said, "I am the way, the truth, and the life." When Jesus said this he might have said "I am the way of acting; I have insight into behavior—why people live like they do, and act like they do; and I have within me the source of life which I can give to men." In John 5:25-26 Jesus says, "The time has already come—when the dead will hear the voice of the

Son of God and those who hear it will live. Even as the Father is himself the source of life in the same way he has made his Son to be the source of life." So, when Jesus says, "I am the life" I think he is really saying "I am the source of life." This gives a richer translation to the Scripture we are considering and makes it possible for us to understand to a greater degree the real intent that Jesus had when he said I am come that ye might have life and when he says on other occasions that he gives life to us. I think this also challenges we who are Christians to consider the fact that when Jesus says "I give you life," he really means that he gives to us the capacity to have within the source of life. On more than one occasion Jesus said that what the Father gave to him he has given to us. In other words, what God sent him to do, he has also sent us to do.

Jesus said "For even as the Father raises the dead back to life, in the same way the Son gives life to those he wants to." Jesus said, "I am the bread of life. He who comes to me will never be hungry. He who believes in me will never be thirsty." I believe the strength of this saying is found in the fact that because he has in him the source of life which does not give out, then no matter how often one comes back to him he will receive food or he will receive drink. This is a characteristic that is true of life givers. No matter how many times one goes back, they always have something to offer.

Still another saying of Jesus which should challenge us is his saying that "Whoever believes in me, streams of living water will pour out from his heart." How can a stream of living water pour out from a person unless the source of that stream is within? So, we sense here that when Jesus says, "I am the way, the truth, and the life," he speaks about life in terms of the eternal source or eternal spring to which there is no end.

Jesus said, "I am the truth." There is an interesting statement found in John 8:32 spoken to the Jews who believed in him. He said, "You will know the truth, and the truth will make you free." It appears Jesus is saying that one will know him who is the truth and will also have insight into his own life and behavior. This means, then, the person who has the truth should be able to see into himself in a clearer fashion. And he also should be able to see into the life and behavior of friends and strangers.

Jesus' promise that "Ye shall know the truth and the truth shall set you free" is a promise that has real meaning only to a life seeker or the life giver. For when he said ye shall have an insight and thus know what is going on, you shall be free. We can conclude from this statement that Jesus is referring to what will happen if an individual gains an insight into himself and then becomes responsible to act on that insight. For it is not just in saying the name, "Jesus Christ," or proclaiming the fact that he is the Son of God that we become free. It is in seeing in the life and behavior of Jesus Christ a new way of acting, a new way of thinking, a new way of feeling that we become free from our old ways of acting, thinking, and feeling. We are, by seeing in behavior its real meaning, free to put down old ways that, do not give life to others and which in many cases destroy the life and personality of others.

On one occasion Jesus answered the Pharisees by saying, "You come from here below, but I come from above. You come from this world, but I do not come from this world. That is why I told you that you will die in your sins. And you will die in your sins if you do not believe that 'I am who I am'." It seems that Jesus is saying to people, "because you come from below and you look at life and at the behavior of men as blind men instead of with truth and insight, then you are bound forever to ways of acting that enslave you. You will continue in the way you act which is in sin until your death overtakes you." He goes on to say that the only way to break a behavior pattern which is a sin or death pattern is to believe the statement which he makes so clearly "I am who I am." When one contemplates the meaning of the words, "I am who I am," he finds that herein is the most appropriate way to describe a human being with personality. No other animal has the capacity to say "I am" and consciously know his existence. Thus, the fact that we are created in the image of God means, that as Jesus can say "I am", so can we say "I am." The dilemma or predicament that man has, and which these Pharisees were having, is that we are unable to say "I am who I am." This is because the sin or human way of life really means I am not myself, but a slave to someone else. Sometimes I am my father. Sometimes I am my mother. Sometimes I am my sister or brother or friend. Too infrequently I am myself.

This may seem strange, but if one reads the Bible in John 8, he finds Jesus telling the Jews what they are trying to do to him. Their behavior toward him is nothing more than the same behavior that their father would do to him. He points out very clearly that if God were really their father these Jews would love him. But because their father in reality is the devil, their behavior is like his which was from the very beginning that of a murderer and a liar. Having told them who their father is, he says to them "I will tell you the truth," (I will give you an insight) this is why you do not believe me."

So we can see that when Jesus says, "I am the truth," he is really saying "I come offering to men insights." In this saying of Jesus we find hope for all men who follow him to be persons who have insight and who can offer their insights to other men.

Jesus said, "I am the way of acting." Now isn't this strange because humanity, if it does anything, acts. Some of its activity is very strange. Much of it is very good. But when Jesus says I am the way of acting, he is saying something about life giving.

Jesus once said, "The Son does nothing on his own; he does only what he sees his father doing. What the father does, the son also does, for the father loves the son and shows him all that he himself is doing. He will show him even greater things than this to do and you will all be amazed" (John 5:19-21). The word that I like best in this statement is "shows" or "show." Jesus said that his father shows him what he's doing and will show him even greater things to do. The striking nature of the words shows and show is seen when put in relationship to a statement which Jesus made to the Pharisees at another time. He said to them, "I talk about what my Father has shown me, but you do what your father has told you." Once again we see that Jesus' way of acting comes from insight—seeing not only what was being done, but understanding the meaning therein. Is it any wonder that during his ministry upon the earth Jesus was able to look quickly at the behavior of the people he encountered and conclude things about them which made them marvel? It should not be amazing to you nor to me for we now know he was able to look within. This we have said before is an essence of the life giving person and a necessary ingredient for successful intervention into the life and ways of others.

The Pharisees, on the other hand, were acting off of rules that had been passed along to them by their fathers, the meanings of which had been left with some distant generation. They, the Jews, were carrying out to the letter what their fathers insisted that they carry out. They were not free to act in any new way but always and only in the same manner that their fathers had told them. We see this even today when men still unthinkingly act in exactly the same fashion their parents acted even when the manner of acting continues to bring destruction, hurt, or failure to them and to the people with whom they live. Life giving is seen when one looks insightfully at the Jesus who said "I am the way, the truth, and the life."

Let's look at some of the life giving experiences in Jesus' life. One that I like very much is when the Jews brought in a woman who had been caught committing adultery. They made her stand before Jesus and told him of her behavior. They reminded him "in our law Moses gave a commandment that such a woman must be stoned to death. Now, what do you say?" Jesus had enough insight to know they said this to trap him. But Jesus, bent over, wrote on the ground with his finger, and meditated while they stood there asking questions. Then he straightened up and gave an insight which caused the Jews to look in a different light at what Moses was supposed to have told them. "Whichever one of you has committed no sin may throw the first stone at her." Then Jesus waited while each of them contemplated his own inadequacies.

We do not know nor can we really guess all that must have gone on inside these men. Of one thing we're sure, however, and that is the truth Jesus gave freed them at least on this occasion from acting the way their fathers had acted many times before and the way they thought Moses through his law had told them to act. They, however, had known the truth and at least momentarily the truth had set them free.

When they were gone Jesus turned to the woman and in his own fashion put a question to her, a question which had insight in it. It was a question that had more answer than it did question. "Where are they, woman? Is there no one left to condemn you?" "No one, Sir," she answered. "Well, then," Jesus said, "I do not condemn you either. You may leave, but do not sin again." In these words Jesus made a woman free to be responsible for her own behavior. It is impossible for you and me to know by what circumstances and events this woman had come to the practice of adultery. We only know that she was carrying out a behavior that had some meaning to her. Imagine how she would have felt if Jesus had said to her "I'll be responsible for you and I'll be responsible for your behavior." But he didn't do this. He simply said, "I cannot condemn you for what you've done." Could it be that Jesus knew she was only trying to live life as she knew how.

Do you suppose Jesus knew that in her early life she had been taught only those ways that led to this behavior? Do you suppose he knew the real source of this destructive behavior was to be found in her father or her father's father? These are only questions that we might ponder. We are certain that he said "I do not condemn you either." In so doing and in dismissing her he surely had given the insight that if she had needs which this behavior called for, she was responsible to see that these needs were met but in a better way. It was to be a way of acting that was not the kind that Adam brought—the kind known as sin, but rather she was to meet her needs responsibly in a way that would be life giving to that person who was a part of her needs meeting.

Another dramatic event occurred in the home of Lazarus—the man Jesus raised from the dead. Jesus was visiting in the home where he had completed dinner. While he was in the home Mary, the sister of Lazarus, took a bottle of very expensive perfume or ointment and as was the custom in those days, poured all of it on Jesus' feet. Then to show her appreciation and love for Jesus she wiped his feet with her hair. One translator says that the sweet smell of the perfume filled the whole house. Judas was upset at the apparent waste of a very expensive perfume which he knew could be converted into money and the money used for many purposes including giving it to the poor. In his upset emotional condition, he asked why the perfume was not sold for $300 and the money given away. Jesus was ready for he already knew that Judas was a man who at heart was greedy and as the Scripture says "a thief." So he responded. It is interesting to note that he really did not offer Judas an insight into himself—into his greediness and into a behavior that Judas surely had learned from his family. He simply responded, "Leave her alone. Let her keep what she has for the day of my burial. You will always have poor people with you, but I will not be with you always." Jesus offered a magnificent insight into human behavior when he showed that there are always people, like Judas, who are trying to keep other people, like Mary, from being who they really are, from acting the way they really are. This life giver deliberately intervened when Judas, who not being able to restrain Mary from her act of love, tried to make her feel that she had done wrong, tried to give her bad feelings, tried to hurt her self esteem. But Jesus' sharp "Leave her alone" accomplished what was intended and caused Judas to step back for Mary was to be allowed to express to Jesus Christ who she really was. He further showed to all of us that it is important for one to be who he is to all kinds of people. It is important for us to love people who already have love, and it is important for us to love people who already have life. Acts of love which are themselves acts of life giving are needed even by the great men of the world and by one great man, especially, who was God.

Jesus gave life in this incident to Mary. He let her go on being and confirmed her in terms of who she was. Don't you imagine that if Jesus had not responded quickly others of the disciples in another moment or two would have joined with Judas in putting Mary down. I can believe that because of the behavior of good men, the disciples of Jesus, in just a little while Mary might have left the room, crying because she was misunderstood.

What do you think about what Jesus did in Jericho? This is one of the times where Jesus chose the rich. He chose the home of Zacchaeus as the place where he would stay. And Zacchaeus, the tax collector, was a very rich man. In fact, because of his wealth and the way he gained his wealth he was also a man much despised by the people of Jericho. They wouldn't have anything to do with him for they saw him as an unjust man who was a sinner. There were questions and eyebrows raised because Jesus went to be a guest in the home of this sinner Zacchaeus. Whatever affect this decision had on other people, it was an intervention that changed the way Zacchaeus saw himself and the way he acted in light of who he was. Jesus' act of simply saying to Zacchaeus "I am willing to be seen with you, I am willing to be identified with you, I am willing to let people know that I can accept you" was all that Zacchaeus needed to see himself as a man who had some value other than as a tax collector.

It is very possible that Zacchaeus, who was a rich man and certainly did not need more money, cheated the people in order to express his anger toward them for the way they treated him as a person. Perhaps he did deserve to be thought of as an evil man, but real life givers would not have treated him so. They would have accepted his need for wealth and his greed as being his problem not theirs, and offered help to him. This is what Jesus did. And when Jesus' behavior said to Zacchaeus "I can accept you the way you are and the way you have been," Zacchaeus could not continue his behavior. The Scripture does not say that he gave up his occupation as a tax collector. It simply says that he intended to change the way he acted and the way he saw things. Wealth that was previously meant for him alone was now wealth that could be shared with the poor. Wealth that he had gained by shrewd dishonest manipulations now was to be returned not in the amount first collected but four times as much. I would say that Zacchaeus was a person who had been given life. He was a new person after Jesus Christ intervened.

Jesus did not always have his insights accepted and acted upon responsively. However, this did not stop him from continuing to offer them. There was, you recall, a rich young ruler who came to Jesus to ask him the way to live and the way to have the source of life within. When Jesus asked if he had kept the word of his fathers, he responded that he had. He answered Jesus in terms that made Jesus know that the youth knew what it meant to steal or lie or dishonor. When Jesus heard his reply, he offered an insight by suggesting that he try a new behavior. "Sell all you have and give the money to the poor. Then you will have riches in Heaven. Then come and follow me." Jesus' insight, the truth which was needed to set the young man free, was the young man's over dependency upon wealth. Very possibly the young man enjoyed the wealth that had been accumulated by his parents. His youthful age would tend to support this view. Perhaps in growing up in his father's house where there was always wealth, the young man had unknowingly become overly dependent upon the way of life that wealth is able to sustain. But in this overdependency, he had become a slave to a style of life. Jesus really never found any problem with money. He even says that we should make a friend of money for it is a means to doing much good and creating a fuller life for ourselves and others. But when money and wealth have become more than our means to a full life, it has become our master. We have become its slave. Jesus said, "ye shall know the truth and the truth shall set you free." But the rich young ruler could not accept the truth. He could not receive it and act upon it. He went away sorrowfully for he knew that with his wealth and the life style his wealth supported he had not achieved the real richness which he knew was a possibility in life.

The event of Peter's denial of Jesus is another example of his capacity to offer life and yet not be dismayed when his life giving offer is not accepted. Jesus had told Peter of the right given to Satan to test Peter (Luke 22:31). He shared with Peter the fact that he had prayed Peter would stand when this test came. But Jesus had an insight into Peter. He knew his humanity. He was aware that Peter lacked strength and insight into his personality. So Jesus said to Peter, "And when you turn back to me, you must strengthen your brothers," referring to the fact that after Peter had denied him and had recovered from this event he was to be a support for those others who would be weak. But Peter would have none of this. He protested saying he was ready to go to prison with Jesus and even to die with him. It was at this moment that Jesus offered him an insight, "I tell you, Peter, the rooster will not crow today until you have said three times that you do not know me." We all know what happened after this. Peter did deny Christ. Yet knowing that this would happen Jesus did not seek to control Peter. He did not try to manipulate him. He only sought to offer life. Peter was unable to accept it on this occasion.

From the study of the Bible and the sayings of Jesus, I have the conviction that Christ intended for those who follow him to be life givers. Paul writes that "for him to live is Christ." This is a further expression of the possibility that lies within the grasp of every believing Christian. Christ himself made references which should challenge us to consider the possibilities that are in each disciple. He said (John 14) "Whoever believes in me will do the works I do. Yes, he will do even greater ones, for I am going to the Father." In these words Christ was trying to show those in every generation who would follow his teachings the possibility in giving the truth to their fellowman. This is further supported by the expression that Christ made in his prayer to God for those he would leave behind in the world. He prayed to God: "Just as I do not belong to the world, they do not belong to the world. Make them your own by means of the truth; your word is truth. I sent them into the world just as you sent me into the world."

In this conversation between the father and the Son nothing needed to be hidden because it was one of the most serious moments in the earthly life of Christ. Jesus reviewed with God his own intention for those of us who are his followers. He accepts as a fact that we are sent into the world just exactly like he was sent into the world.

As I contemplate this prayer my mind rushes back to the words recorded in John 3:16, "For God so loved the world that he gave his only begotten Son that whosoever believeth in him should not perish. . . ." This is why Christ was sent into the world.

I hear the words, "I am come that you might have life in complete fulness." This is why Jesus was sent into the world. "Ye shall know the truth and the truth shall make you free." This is why Jesus was sent into the world. Again, Jesus said, "I tell you the truth: whoever obeys my message will never die." He said, "I am the resurrection and the life. Whoever believes in me will live even though he dies. And whoever lives and believes in me will never die." For this reason, Jesus was sent into the world.

So as we recall these truths about why Jesus came to us in the world, we must be constrained by the belief that we are to be something other than mere men. We are to be Life Givers. In Christ we are created a new species. We are made in his image, and as such should be found as life giving spirits. The fulfilment of this possibility is a combination of our faith and our skill. For in knowing Christ we have experienced the results of life giving, and we have within us the Source of Life. The spirit of Truth is our companion, teaching us not only those things Jesus left for men to understand, but teaching us all things which we may need to fulfil his mission among men. Our hurting world demands that we hold steadfastly to the conviction that through men God is making available his grace. Perishing people call us to believe that men of Christ are not only instruments of peace, instruments of good will, but are also instruments of life giving.

FOUR

THE LIFE GIVER

Why do people with problems turn to certain people for help and ignore resources that other people have? Another way to raise this question is to ask, "Why are some people readily seen as life givers whereas other people live out their life without ever being called upon to help people solve their innermost problems?" Perhaps the best way to understand the nature of a life giver is to consider him from the standpoint of a person who himself is in need of help. This should be fairly easy since at one time or another everyone of us has needed help—help that we could not supply ourselves—help that we had to go beyond ourselves to gain.

Oftentimes when a person with a problem is seeking help, he is not quite certain how to describe the problem. Obviously he does not see clearly all of the aspects that are in the problem. He lacks the freedom from involvement so he can objectively analyze the situation and consider alternatives in solving the problem. Perhaps he is so involved that he does not see certain factors contributing to the problem. This is especially true when an individual has to cope with a problem in which there is a great deal of emotion or where there are very close relationships to other people involved.

The person with a problem looks for someone whom he feels

will keep in confidence those aspects of the problem which he does not want public. Keeping a confidence requires discipline far beyond the capability of the average person. All one has to do is listen to what is being said in the places one goes. One will find people telling what their friends have told them. Inadvertently they will give out information which a thoughtful person would readily recognize should be kept secret, or if shared, should be done so discreetly.

But our world lives off of the information of misery. The old saying, "misery loves company," is as true today as ever. Many people find that passing along information about the troubles of others is one way to gain attention and to keep their minds off of their own problems. The person who wants to share himself fully with another person in order to gain that person's help does not want to be careful about what he says. He wants to feel free and comfortable in sharing with another. If he is afraid what he has to say will be repeated, then he is hesitant to share it.

A person with a problem likes to get help from someone whom he feels will listen with the intent of understanding. We often see people who listen to another person talk only in order to have his time to talk back. Have you ever observed groups of people in conversation? Have you noticed which ones listen? I have a friend who very seldom says anything in a group. He believes that being quiet means one is listening and a listener is always the wisest person. There is some truth in his position.

However, there is far more to be said for the person who listens *and* understands. I have tested many individuals in groups to discover if they are understanding what they hear or just listening to words. Recently, a group of friends and I tested ourselves. It was shocking for several to discover that, although they were listening to what was being said, they really could not accurately repeat what they had heard. This was, of course, also an evidence they did not understand clearly all that was being said.

Some people who are good listeners, quiet and attentive, may wonder why people say they must be wise and thoughtful and yet do not come to them to get help for their problems. It is probably because people needing help have discovered that, though they appeared to be listening, these people were not accurately hearing what was being said nor were they understanding the meanings which were being conveyed.

A person with a problem always wants to get help from a person who is forgiving. This may seem strange since a person who has been asked for help is not actually a person who is part of the problem. But when people have problems they cannot solve, they often blame themselves for the problem or for certain parts of it. Their guilt is twofold. They feel guilty because they have the problem, and sometimes they feel guilty because they cannot solve it alone. Obviously a person who is being asked for help knows that he is not God and is not the one to forgive another for a sin not committed against him. However, his attitude must reflect a feeling that if this person were his enemy or the cause of a problem, he would be willing to understand and forgive. This kind of attitude provides for the seeking person an atmosphere in which he does not have to cope with increased guilt or anxiety. In other words, a life giver does not add to those feelings of guilt and anxiety which a person may already have. We are perhaps most like Christ when we are able to hear people without condemning them. I believe it was the intention of God to put us at ease when in the book of John we read the words about Jesus which say he came not into the world to condemn the world. Also notice what he said when the elders brought the woman who had been caught in adultery. Jesus said to her "No man condemns you and therefore, I will not condemn you either." Such responses in us today have an unbelievable positive effect upon people who come to share their innermost problems.

If these are the kinds of things a person with a problem looks for when he is seeking help, how do we describe a person who is a life giver? *A life giver is one who honestly esteems every person no matter what the person is, is doing, or has done. Life givers see people as they can be, not as he must make them, not as he needs them to be.*

Perhaps the highest virtue, one never attained, is to esteem every person we meet. Humanity perverts this virtue in two ways. Sometimes we esteem persons without ever knowing them. There is no difference between one man and another. Now, having said we should seek to esteem every person, we should not see every person the same. By blindly acting like every person is identical, we may develop a defense mechanism which actually says we don't care deeply about people. We don't care deeply enough to esteem them as individuals nor to know them as individuals. On the other hand, there are those who find it impossible to give respect to certain categories of persons or to individuals who do not come up to their own standards. Either of these perversions is a block in the pathway to being successful life givers.

We are all humanity. We all encounter evil. We all succumb to evil or we are succumbed by evil. The value of a human being is not found in his condition of life but in the nature of his creation. God made him. Because God made man, he has value. He has value enough to expect the esteem of every other man. Who has made any of us God that we might choose to esteem one man and to say to another man that he has no value? I know this problem is one that will last as long as humanity is humanity. Some men will never be able to judge a man's value except by what he is, is doing, or has done.

We can thank God that always among us are people, life givers, who have the capacity to see within us what we are and what we can be. How often has anyone talked for a moment, ten minutes, or an hour about what you might become? This is a unique occurrence. Most of us can count on one hand the times in our life when this has happened. The life giver is one who has the capacity to see possibilities in persons when all others around see impossibilities. The life giver is one who can accept persons when others have already begun to reject the same person.

The life giver is one who can see possible solutions to other people's problems. He may see these so clearly that he could offer to a person a detailed solution to a problem, but the life giver knows that he must not take over the responsibility for the life of another. We lose our life giving power when we begin to use it to make others like we need them to be or to make them act as we need them to act. Such behavior is manipulation. It destroys the very essence of healthy personality. It denies the right and responsibility of a person to live his own life successfully.

This is most frequently seen in parent-child relationships. I have seen immense hurt result from parents' failure to allow their children to become themselves. Children growing up in this radically changing world of ours have been confronted with problems which those of older generations have never had to face. We tend to think, as parents, that this world is just like the one in which we grew up. Many parents need their children to behave just like they behaved. In insisting upon their children acting like the parent needs them to act, they violate one of the most important aspects of growing up. For though parents are responsible for their children, they are responsible for their children becoming adults.

What are adults? They are people who have become responsible to meet their own needs.

This is why God gave children parents. The infant if left without parents or other responsible adults would soon die for he is completely dependent upon them to meet his needs. But the growth stages from infancy to childhood through the teen years to adulthood should reflect differences in parent-child relationship. Parents should guide their children to independence not to a lifelong dependency relationship. Thus life is planned so children can grow to adulthood by gradually gaining their independence. It appears that the most threatening period of development for parents is during their child's teen-age years. These are the last years when dependency is needed, and the years when independency should be given. No one can gain his independence in one day and use it successfully. Healthy growing up is the gradual increase of independence from one's parents. Some parents like to think that the children in their home should behave exactly as the parents need for them to behave until the day they leave to make their own living and their own home. I have never met children who grew up in such a home who did not have some kind of problem.

Many parents cannot get over the myth that they are going to raise perfect children. Children are going to do evil. Children are going to make mistakes. This is how they learn. This is how they grow. This may be the way they die. But it is the only way for them to come to healthy adulthood. In the effort to overprotect children from the evil of their world, one may come dangerously close to becoming the greatest evil in their world.

Life givers have learned a lesson from such parents. They know that to take over responsibility in order to meet one's own need is to fail in efforts to help others.

Seeing possibility in persons is a skill the life giver can develop. A friend of mine is doing excellent work in a position which he was recently given. The competency with which he is doing his work has come as a surprise. Many felt that he was incompetent for the work. They saw the following weaknesses: a weakness in relating well to others, a weakness of meeting his own needs before meeting the needs of others, a weakness of being trained in another field, and a weakness of not being practical in some aspects of the work. These were just a few. Fortunately for this man and others, some people saw the possibility in his strengths. Today he is a man who does his work with certain weaknesses, but his strengths far overshadow his weaknesses. Through the life giving relationships which he has with others, his weaknesses become less important obstacles than before.

I remember Jimmy, a mentally retarded youngster. In the summer when he could get about by himself, he would come by the office. He wanted attention. He wanted to be somebody. To many he was a nuisance. He was bothersome. They saw in him his impossibility. Others of us saw Jimmy in his possibility. Soon we had him doing those things which he was capable of doing. He was able to succeed when the tasks were within his range. Mentally retarded persons need self-respect, need to know they are of value, and need to contribute to their world. Mental retardates like all of us need life givers.

Seeing possibility in some situations is a matter of faith. Once in response to a newspaper article which I had written, a man called. He told me that he and his wife were in the process of getting a divorce. He described the kind of help they had sought. He said very frankly that he did not think there was any hope for the marriage to be saved, but that he and his wife were willing to make one more try. Shortly they were in my study. The story they told is not different from the kind which we all know something about. They had hurt one another in every way and with every method possible. These people had used words. They had used fists. They had used feelings. They had even used objects to express their anger, distrust, and hopelessness to one another.

I listened to their story to understand who they were and why they could not find a basis for relating. It became apparent that the husband lacked the capacity to trust any woman. It had grown out of his earlier experiences with an unfaithful mother. Therefore, he was suspicious and distrusting of all things his wife did which he did not understand. His feelings of suspicion and distrust were expressed toward her without opportunity for her to explain. Obviously, even if she had explained, it would have not been adequate since the basis of the problem was within him. This was a problem he had never told her about, a problem that he thought existed only between himself and his mother. As time passed, this couple gained the insight that the angry battle begun between this man and his mother was now reaching a greater intensity of destruction between him and his wife. Interestingly, this man still loved his wife. Probably he sensed her fighting was more to save their marriage than it was to destroy him. She saw in him the hurt person that he was. She was able to see again the possibility she had first seen in their marriage. He came to understand why she could fight so intensely for she was one who cared. So, through patience, understanding, lots of prayer, and a life giving effort, an impossible situation became possible. This family has until now lived not only in harmony but with a strange sense of existence because they know who they are and the price they have paid to be together.

A life giver is one who understands. He not only understands a person in terms of feelings such as anger, fear, hope or joy, he understands that people do get in trouble. He understands that evil is a problem for every man. He understands that people have their own way of getting into trouble. He listens in order to understand what problem a person has and to learn how he came to have the problem. Quite often people who need help will give information regarding their need which they themselves do not hear. I have a friend who is a real life giver. He has an above-average capacity to listen for meanings. He observes the tone of voice, facial expression, condition of eyes, words used, and body movement. He listens to understand. Sometimes while listening to a person describe his problem my friend will suddenly stop him and say, "Did you hear what you said?" The individual usually a bit taken aback seeks momentarily to recall things he has been saying. But, because he was lost in the telling, is not able to repeat what has just been said. On such occasions my friend may say, "I heard you say. . . ." At this point he will repeat what was said and say, "This is what I understand you to be saying."

Quite often the individual in amazement says, "I never knew that's what I meant!" Such occasions are often the moments of truth—the time when an insight which has been escaping a person comes. We need to listen for meanings. We wrongly assume that all the communication that is taking place occurs through the use of words. The observant life giver knows that quite often much more is revealed by looking at behaviors other than talking.

The cheeks are normally excellent communicators of feeling. Anger brings a flush of pink or red. Fear causes a paleness. Normal color may be a defense mechanism. Eyes also say more than most people realize for they tell us how troubled a person is. They show hurt at its deepest level. They become cloudy as the mind contemplates a hopeless situation. They become bright when there is joy upon remembrance or anticipation. They become tearful when the person is turning strong feelings into himself or sorrows at the memory of some previous hurt.

The life giver speaks the language of thought, feeling, and action, but especially the language of feeling. I have been intrigued with an experiment that I sometimes try in conversation with people. I ask what they *feel* about a given situation. They will respond by saying "I think" or they will describe what they think about the situation. Having finished the sentence, I oftentimes repeat, "But how do you feel about this?" Again they will respond with reason and rational answers to my question about feelings. On some occasions I have put the question to a person the fourth time and fifth time before asking him if he had an emotional vocabulary. It is true that many people do not have a vocabulary for expressing feelings. It has been an exciting experience to help some people learn to use feeling words.

Have you ever taught a child to say new words? It's almost the same. Such people must be handed words, told what they mean, told what their meaning is, and allowed to try them on. As adults or teen-agers, you can imagine that they must feel a bit silly, and they do. Developing the use of a new word that reflects one's feelings is very strange indeed. How can a person convey to another all aspects of his problem if his vocabulary is inadequate. There are homes in which children grow up that have very limited vocabularies for expressing feelings. This is especially true of a vocabulary to express negative feelings.

There are many homes, Christian homes, where love is understood to be a positive feeling. This is a misconception. Love is a relationship; it is the quality of a relationship. A love relationship is one in which a person, or two persons, have a commitment to one another. It may be a commitment between mother and child, brother and sister, husband and wife, or friends. *But it is a relationship of commitment.* This relationship if healthy, experiences all types of feelings and successfully incorporates these feelings into its being. Many people are surprised to learn that love includes anger and fear as well as joy and affection. Parents or spouses often realize that they are angry toward or fearful for the one to whom they are committed, but they feel that this is a weakness in their love. It is something which cannot be tolerated or allowed. Many homes build their whole relationship on the principle that negative feelings have no place there. But the feelings of anger and fear are given to us by God for a purpose. They must be allowed to live and do their work.

Anger is the feeling that warns us when an injustice is being done, or is possibly being done, to our personalities. Anger is like a bell that rings. In addition to warning about the possible injustice, anger also creates the energy needed to confront the cause of injustice and correct it. Many people think anger is evil because they do not know the difference between the feeling of anger, which is a friend, and undisciplined, uncontrolled ways of expressing anger. Anger may be expressed in many ways. It can be expressed with acceptable behaviors; or it may be expressed with unacceptable behaviors. Anger as a feeling may be recognized by a person, accepted for what it means, and not expressed at all. We must come to see that anger has a right to exist and if denied will cause serious damage to our personalities and lives. Fear is the feeling which God has given us to warn that we are in danger of losing our existence. Fear does not say we are going to lose our existence, it only warns us that we are in danger. In fact, it does not even judge whether the danger is real or imagined. It leaves that to our reason. When it clamors for attention, we should listen. Having heard its call for attention we must use our reasoning capacity to determine what method we shall use to express our fear.

Mankind has been a feeling species since the beginning. Doesn't it strike you as being peculiar that man understands his feelings so inadequately? Isn't it even more difficult to realize that many men do not have an adequate vocabulary by which they can successfully express feelings in all situations. One reason man has not developed the ability to speak his feelings is that his community or society are afraid to give him this privilege. We are all afraid of undisciplined, uncontrolled behavior. We know what it can do. Since we normally associate undisciplined, uncontrolled behavior with undisciplined and uncontrolled feelings, we put undue restraints upon ourselves. It is true that many people who have negative feelings use them destructively in a violent fashion against other people. It is not true that all people who have negative feelings are so undisciplined or uncontrolled. On the other hand, we seldom ever stop to count the damage done to personalities and personal relationships because feelings are not adequately expressed. Mental institutions are filled with the people who are unable to adequately express either their positive or negative feelings. It is time that we properly assessed the damage and destruction being done to human life by those who are unable to express their feelings. We need also to seek to understand those people who express their feelings in an undisciplined manner.

The life giver should also speak the language of thought. He must be able to give, as we have said earlier, meanings to the person who is seeking help. These meanings must be expressed in the form of ideas. It is appalling how often people who are in trouble with problems they cannot solve are unable to think up and propose alternate solutions to their problems. They often protest they cannot think at all or their ideas have no value. The life giver is one who not only can reason and develop alternative solutions to problems, but by doing so he can show others how to develop their own alternatives to problems. Obviously, if the life giver has a great need to be needed, he may stop short of developing in another person the capacity to solve problems. Nevertheless, by offering several practical ideas without prejudicing a person to take the "right" one, a person can remain a successful life giver.

Actions speak louder than words. This is a saying with which we are all familiar, but we do not always recognize the positive value in it. The statement is generally used to threaten people into changing the way they are doing. Whatever the reason, the statement is pretty true. Therefore, we need to understand behavior; not just react to it. We need to use actions in addition to words to communicate meanings. Recently, in a tense situation, some persons were having difficulty understanding the deep hurt others were experiencing. Having tried several times with words to convey this feeling to the individual, I finally decided that actions might speak better than words. I left my chair, crossed the room, and without warning stomped with some force the foot of this person. He immediately reacted and said that it hurt. I asked him to contemplate the hurt that he was experiencing. He did so. For the first time he became emotionally aware of the fact that others can hurt and hurt deeply from what other people do. There are many behaviors which convey better than words what is meant. The life giver is one who has learned these and uses them well. In addition, he has developed his own repertoire of actions to help people who have problems.

The life giver is one who loves truth as much as he loves life. The reason he has this great commitment to truth is because he knows that life at its very best is lived where truth is of the highest value. He understands the Scripture quoted earlier that "Ye shall know the truth, and the truth shall set you free." A search for truth is an exciting activity, but it is also fearful and sometimes hurtful. It is because of man's experience in searching for truth that the common sense proverb, "truth hurts," was developed. Truth does hurt, but truth also gives life. For this reason, the life giver is forever in search of it.

The life giver's search for truth is far more than just a search for facts. It is a truth of life that the more deeply involved we are in a situation, the more difficult it becomes for us to understand it and see the meanings in it. A life giver searches for insight and offers this insight to others. I have seen people use facts to complicate a problem, confuse the problem solvers, or even punish and destroy those who would solve a problem.

A father and son were in deep conflict over a course which the father wanted the son to take in college. The son had reached a point of being adamant and rebellious toward his father when the subject was brought up. The father pursued the son with facts. First he pointed out how important this particular course was in order to supply the son with a complete university education. Secondly, he pointed to the fact that the son's intelligent quotient and other measures of his ability showed that he could easily master the subject matter. He also brought out the fact that the son had taken similar type courses. In fact he had previously taken the same course in an elementary form and had done well in it. These facts formed a concrete logic which the father used to argue incessantly with his son. These were facts. Had they been all the truth in this situation they would have justified perhaps the father's insistence. However, the son looked at the problem differently.

He wanted university to be an experience that helped him along the road to becoming himself. If he followed the narrow path set forth in the curriculum which he was by test best qualified to complete, he might do quite well academically and even get a good education in that field. Somehow the youngster looked at the university differently. He saw it as an opportunity to find out who he wanted to be by trying out some courses of study which did not closely fit his life style. This appeared to be foolish to this father. So, for the son the conflict became a battle to be. If he were to relinquish to his father's wish, then he would be taking a course to meet his father's need. At the same time he would be denying his own need to explore. Had this problem not been solved adequately, I am certain the son would eventually have relinquished to his father. But having done so he probably would have performed very poorly making low grades even to the possibility of failing the course. An insight the father needed was that the son needed to be himself. He needed the opportunity of experimenting or exploring without fear in order to find himself.

It is much better for a young person to fail a course in an area such as engineering than to wait until later in life and fail in the vocation of engineering because he was not allowed to explore it. In other words, taking a course in college which allows a person to find out his interest and capability is a relatively inexpensive and practical way for a youth to discover that he does or doesn't want to be something. I have given help to parents and their children who in college flunked all courses in a semester of work. Some of this could be judged as being the best thing to have happened. In other cases, it appears that mass and continuous failures are the result of a youngster who could not find himself. He was going to school to meet his parent's need or while enjoying school he was having difficulty in knowing who he would become.

In the above case the life giver offered the father and son an insight as to what the real argument was about. He discussed the real needs of the father and the real needs of the son. In such a situation, the motivations that caused each to want to control this situation became clear. As usually happens, when the truth was out, they each were in a position to work together for the best conclusion. This they did.

The father recognized that even though it hurt, he had to give the son an opportunity to be responsible. This meant an opportunity to become himself. The son, on the other hand, sensed how much his father wanted him to succeed, not just for success but that he might have life. In the conflict of ideas and feelings the father had given signals that he needed the son to do the father's wishes in order for the father to be successful. As you can see this caused the son to wonder whether he was important. On the other hand, because the son reacted openly and aggressively the father felt that his authority was being questioned and that the son was losing respect for him. They both hurt as they searched, but out of the encounter came something more than just the right decision about a university course. The truth gave life to a deeper and better relationship between father and son.

The life giver believes in openness and honesty. Openness and honesty describes an atmosphere, an environment, a climate. Unfortunately, it is a climate in which few are privileged to live out the whole of their lives. And there are many who never experience for any length of time a climate of openness and honesty. The reason that the life giver seeks to create a climate of openness and honesty is because he knows this is where truth has the best opportunity to exist. Undisciplined expression of fear is probably the greatest enemy to openness and honesty. People whose fears set their imaginations and behaviors running rampant are not willing to tolerate anything which might stimulate or create fear feelings. Therefore, such people are always trying to control their environment. The object of this control is to keep the world their size and shape so they can live adequately within it. Such people do not tolerate certain ideas being expressed. They will not accept certain words or language being expressed. They are unwilling for certain groups of people to express themselves. They set out specific ways in which an individual can respond—a child to a parent, a wife to a husband, a close friend to a close friend, and a stranger to a stranger. In such rule bound environments people find it difficult to be themselves. Some may even find it impossible to be themselves. When people express themselves freely and truthfully, they provoke a reaction of fear in others that often makes them wish the subject had not opened. Fear people will always be with us, and because of that, will always be trying to control the environment in which they live rather than allow openness and honesty. Life givers cannot tolerate such an environment for themselves and for the people who come to them for help. They know that health and growth will come best in a climate of openness and freedom. Life givers know that a climate of openness and honesty will create problems for people, especially fear people. In their commitment to help people grow, to help people find adequate solutions to their problems, they work with all of their energy to create a climate which best contributes to this.

On the other hand, I know some people who are committed to openness and honesty more than they are committed to life itself. This is unwise, for when we commit ourselves to openness and honesty as the end, we fail to see that it can also be a means of destruction. A friend of mine insisted beyond need that openness and honesty exist where he was. In insisting upon this, he actually became a controlling person. He controlled to get openness. This person would often insist upon all the facts being brought out into the open or that everybody be completely honest. There is a place for privacy in every life. All the facts may not be necessary to solve a problem, give help, or be a life giver. Life givers sense the propriety of letting a person determine to what extent he can use the climate of openness and honesty which the life giver offers.

When this is done, a person will share all that is needed in order for one to assist him as requested.

I know a person who lives in a climate of openness and honesty. She has created this climate by being open and honest herself. This has been accomplished by the continuous sharing of herself with others. She lets them know who she really is. In her efforts to share herself she has opened her experiences in all areas of life. She has shared experiences of deep hurt which have caused her inner anguish and pain. She has energetically told of exciting joyful experiences with other people. She has talked about experiences of life and death. She has told about inconsequential things like love for her school's football team. This person likes other people as they are. She is never offended by what they say or do, nor is she offended by the way they say it or do it. People feel at home with her. In fact, most people feel better with her than they do at home. By sharing herself in terms of failures as well as successes she has become a very believable person. The interesting way in which she can unobtrusively share in an experience at exactly the right moment is a wonderful skill she has developed. Without knowing it, people become more open and honest when they are around her. Just a few weeks ago this person was with a person who needed to share with someone else the strong feelings he had. It was difficult for him to be open and honest in the way he felt. The fear of rejection was extremely strong. Who was the person he finally talked to? Of course, it was this person who is a model of openness and honesty.

Openness and honesty is more than method. It is much more than the technique of a teacher, minister, or counselor. Openness and honesty is an integral part of the life giving personality.

The life giver is one who pursues his offer to help. There are many people about us who are in need of help. Great numbers of these want help. They are looking for it, but they do not know how to take it. Since they are busy day and night giving signals that they need and want help, it is appropriate for the life giver to take seriously their subconscious invitation to help. When the life giver responds, he often finds that the first offer of help cannot be received. He recognizes that this is not because the individual does not want or need help, but because the individual does not know how to accept help. It is for this reason that the life giver must be willing to pursue such an individual in his offer of help.

Several years ago I met a person. In subsequent experiences of being together, this individual began to indicate verbally her need for help. However, it was not an open request for help but those indirect subtle comments which most of us have the capacity to recognize. On occasion I responded gently and in a subtle manner. I supported the individual's conclusion that she needed help.

After some time, the person sensed that I would be willing to help with the problem if she would take the initiative. The conversation changed as she tried to make me responsible for her coming. I met her half way by acknowledging I was willing to give help but that I was unwilling to force my help upon her. At this stage she turned away. For some time she continued to live with the problem she was having. After some months had passed she again signaled her need for help. This time with a bit more abruptness I pointed out that the help was available. I told her she need not fear the helper or the outcome of getting help. In other words, I began to deal with why she was unable to depend upon other people to help with her problem. This I felt was necessary for it is a common human ailment. There are so many who are trying to live adult lives without depending upon anyone. Or if they depend upon someone then it is those in their own household. Oftentimes, these are the people who are either creating the problem or actively engaged in the problem one has. As I spoke to this person about being too self-reliant, she began to acknowledge a desire to move from conversation to a more serious presentation of her problem. But this meant setting a specific time. Once again she began to withdraw. I began to feel like helpers always feel at such a time. Was it something in me? Whose responsibility was it? If she wants my help, she can come and get it! These and other ideas could have caused me to draw away. But I am not self-sufficient. I know the feelings of rejection, the feelings of insecurity that every person knows. In spite of these I drew myself together and pursued. On this occasion a phone call and a note expressing continued interest was used with an emphasis on the need for this individual to take action in order to receive help. It was almost a year and a half before she finally came. The effort was worth it. The results were better than hoped for. It taught me that the life giver must not give up easily if he is to be successful in offering help.

The life giver not only pursues his offer to help, but he also pursues in giving the help. Have you ever noticed how people with problems are sometimes much more able to live with a problem than take help in solving their problem? Such behavior seems to result from their unwillingness to be responsible for themselves. So they will seek help. They look at help that is offered. They toy with help that is offered. They carry help that is offered home and sleep on it. They discuss with other people the help that has been offered. But using help offered is another thing. Since a life giver, who has been asked for help, has the right to expect an acceptance or rejection of help, he sometimes must pursue with patience and skill. I have previously said that a life giver must not need to make the other person like himself or make him do as the life giver wants him to do. Therefore it is not for these reasons that one pursues. It is in order to help an individual change his situation.

I have observed some people who having already clearly before them the alternatives in solving their problems, took months to act. These people are not only wasting their time but their life.

Therefore, the pursuit of the individual is to gain a decision to act. The life giver does not pursue to get affirmative acceptance of the help offered, but a response that will allow the relationship between the two to progress.

Are life givers God? No. Are life givers professionally trained people? Not necessarily. Life givers are ordinary people who are found in ordinary places doing ordinary things. But how do you find life givers? The people who know them tell you that there's something different about them. Sometimes this difference causes people in the community to reject and despise them, but real life givers always have friends who will stake their life on them. I have been fortunate in coming to know many life givers. Some of these taught school. Some were professional people such as lawyers, doctors, or dentists. Others have operated service stations or grocery stores. Life givers may be stenographers or executives. They may be mothers or teen-agers.

Life giving is a gift. It is a gift that can be improved and developed. It is a gift that God has given to some as a result of the experiences which they have had in life. Some of the finest life givers I have known were ministers, church leaders, and Christians. I have known some life givers who were not church goers and who did not know that they were offering to others the teachings of Christ. In John it is written that God is no respecter of persons. It appears that when it comes to life givers, God has distributed this gift freely to all kinds of people.

The magnificent thing about life givers is how they hold our world together. At the very beginning of this book I described this perishing world of ours. I described people like you and me who are coming apart. We know that whenever a person lives for any length of time there is hurt and problems. There will never be enough trained ministers, trained psychiatrists, trained psychologists, or trained school teachers to care for these hurts and help with the problems of all men. The only way there could be enough of these would be for all men to train for these vocations. This is impossible.

So ordinary men must do the job. They must do it in such a way that others are made whole. We need people to become life givers; life givers who can honestly esteem every person no matter what the person is, is doing, or has done. We need life givers who see people as they can be but not as the life giver must make them.

FIVE

Just Ordinary People

An ordinary couple is all we'll ever be. These words from a song in the musical, *The Sound of Music* causes one to think this couple has nothing about which to be excited or thrilled. However, when listening to the song as it is sung by well-trained voices, one senses the truly exhilarating experience that comes to an ordinary couple who know who they are, what they want, and where they are going.

Life givers are ordinary people. They do extraordinary things. However, the entire purpose of this book would be defeated if I were to leave you with the idea that the performances of life givers is dependent upon advanced educational degrees or that only people of a certain level of proficiency are able to be life givers. Thank goodness this is not true. People of all walks of life, all ages, and all levels of educational training are today engaged in bringing life to others. Perhaps you are one of these. If not, perhaps it is time that you became one of these. Have you ever stopped to look at the people around you and to ask which are taking more from their world than they are putting into it? Have you ever analyzed the siutation in which you live to discover which people have particular ways in which they contribute to the growth and health of others around them? The following people are just

74

a few whom I know and have chosen to illustrate that life givers are ordinary people who do extraordinary things.

Earlier I tried to make the point that we cannot help every person. It appears that a life giver is able to respond to the needs of certain kinds of people whereas he may lack the ability to even maintain a healthy relationship with certain others. Life givers have their way of giving life. Each one develops a method or an approach to giving life which is uniquely his. Sometimes persons who are life givers are able to develop more than one approach and more than one reservoir of strength which they can share. The illustrations which follow will show some of the strengths which these life giving persons have and illustrate their method of making this strength available to others.

Mrs. Spott is a middle-aged person. She is a home keeper with grown children. She has been active for many years in the life of her church and in community activities. She is a very outgoing person, liked by almost everyone who knows her. A few people feel she gets into other people's business too often. Mrs. Spott might be described as an optimist. She encourages people no matter what their problem. She will seldom leave hurting people alone. If necessary, she will share with them over the telephone, by card, or by a visit to their home. You would think that such a person could become obnoxious, particularly if an individual wanted to be alone with their problems. Not so in the case of Mrs. Spott. She causes people to share the things within them which they are having difficulty handling alone. She herself has to offer encouragement she has learned from the Bible and from her own life. I can hear the way she says to people, "You can get help. Let me help you." With these words she oftentimes gets a hurting person to talk to another friend of hers or to see a doctor, minister, pastoral counselor, or psychologist. She believes in all of these people. She believes that one person can help another. I cannot count on my two hands the people to whom this person has been a life giver this year.

Batey Reese is an exceptionally insightful person. He grew up on a farm where things were pretty rough. He managed, in spite of poverty, to educate himself. His parents were very strict. They interpreted the limits of behavior in the most conservative way. Their use of the Bible approached Phariseeism although these parents were very affectionate and loving in their home and to their children. Batey left the home atmosphere to go away to college where he found himself out of place. Thirty years have gone by and now he is an employee of a manufacturing firm. He is well-adjusted and successful in his work. Moreover, he has learned from the experiences of growing up in an overprotected home and having to make his own life in an underprotected world. He gets great enjoyment from offering insights to other people who are still children inside even though they're grown on the outside. He has a thorough knowledge of the Scriptures and is often able to give people an opportunity to become free by showing them things in the Bible which they haven't understood before.

One insight he learned and particularly enjoys sharing is that of the older brother in the parable of the prodigal son. Most people have understood this parable more from the experiences and learnings of the prodigal son than they have from the older brother. My friend points out that the older brother had lived within his father's house as a slave, and the Scripture records the brother's complaint. He, with his father's wealth at his disposal waits throughout his life for his father to tell him how he can use his wealth. The father is shocked to discover how the older brother has assumed this attitude. He tries to tell him the wealth he had accumulated was available to the older brother for his use any way he wanted to use it.

There are a lot of older brothers in our world. These people live in the midst of resources at their disposal. But they fail to see they are free to utilize these to make their own life abundant or to share in making the lives of other people abundant. This friend of mine is a life giver to people who insist on living in poverty.

Lynn is a young person. She is vivacious, full of life. Everywhere she goes she makes things happen. A day for her goes on forever. Wherever she is with people, she is trying to get them to accept an insight which she learned many years ago. She could say it like this, "I love life." She does love life, every part of it. She loves to think, she loves to sing, she loves to share, she loves to challenge, and she loves to plan. More than these, she loves to be. Although she has not yet determined the vocation she will follow, she knows she will be on the side of people. Caught in the privacy of a friend's problem, she does not hesitate to ask them to share it. She has the capacity of causing people to trust her so that they are able to share more than they would with other people. Sometimes she finds herself in over her head. Admitting this is sometimes difficult for her. But when she does, she turns to maturer people she respects to get help for her friends. She is a person who helps through her very being. The animation of her mind and body and feeling are like a symphony. People in her presence learn the tune. Many young people . . . and not a few old . . . have learned new ways of thinking, feeling, and acting from being with this person.

The Browns like to entertain. The entertainment setting is their place for life giving. I've been in their home for dinner many times. Mrs. Brown serves a marvelous meal. She and her husband are intelligent people, but very subtle in the use of their intelligence. Their parties bring together different people. Many of whom have not met before. The subjects they discuss are always of interest to their guests. They have the capacity of getting people to discuss an issue in an objective way. The natural ease with which they can put a question on a controversial social or political issue is a beautiful behavior to observe. They have led parents to see their ridiculous attitude about some teen-age behavior. They have caused some teen-agers to recognize their insensible rebellious behavior toward their parents. The thing which most characterizes their life giving is described by the words "climate of openness." Wonderful Christians, who grew up in the midst of traditional biblical teachings, they have become a bridge to people in the world and people of the world.

Candid is the way to describe how Pat gives life. He is a young man in the management of a rather large company. He grew up in a family where conflict was accepted as a normal thing. He learned that facing facts ultimately was the best way out of a problem. Some people have difficulty relating to Pat. Others who relate to him on the surface cannot handle his frank approach when he offers them personal help. He tells it like it is. Not everyone could do this because most of us lack the ability to collect facts, analyze them, and offer succinctly the meaning of what we have found. Pat is a master of this. Integrity is the key word in Pat's life. When he sees disintegration taking place in a person he has to offer life.

Charlie was a porter in a company for which I worked. Like many porters, he was a philosopher. Like many porter philosophers, he had distilled insights from his own life which he could offer to others. A congenial person, Charlie had developed his way of offering people insights. They were in sayings which sounded to the listener like humor, but upon contemplation one often found a pearl of great price. One of these which characterizes Charlie's method and message of life giving went like this: A male employee had just reminded Charlie that it was not his job to think but to do. Charlie observed to me, "Some people don't want others to think cause it reminds them that they don't!" This and other insights from Charlie have helped make my life and the lives of scores of other employees richer than before. He has been an aid in overcoming prejudice. He made me realize that many people who have been denied equal opportunity have, in spite of this, developed the capacity to be life givers to their whole world. Unlike Lynn, Charlie is the kind of person you have to be around awhile. His own hurt in life causes him to be hesitant to offer life to just anyone. Nevertheless, he goes on trying. As one's relationship to Charlie grows, so his activity of life giving grows.

I don't know when Kay first realized she was somebody, and I'm not certain when she realized that being somebody was great. She was almost thirty when I met her. She was my teacher, but she was far more than a school teacher. She was a life giver. The life she offered can be summed up in the words "It's great to be somebody." I've never met anyone who was more committed to the magnificent obsession that the greatest thing in the world is to be somebody. Kay knew herself, knew who she was and what she could do. She felt at ease with everyone she met, and felt competent to deal with any problem. Kay tried to get everyone to accept the greatness of being somebody. Because she worked so hard at it, I sometimes felt her behavior was artificial. But looking at the results of this person's life, I have to acknowledge that she was real. Many students whom Kay taught came from the lower economic section of our city. They were people who felt themselves to be of little value and who had been taught to conceive of themselves as people of low esteem. Most would end up doing work that called for little imagination and very little creative professionalism. But Kay changed self-concepts and, in changing self-concepts, she changed lives. Today many people who would have gone through life thinking of themselves as nobody are now somebody. They are not only somebody to themselves and their families, but they are somebody to their community and to their world. This life giver had insight and developed the capacity to give this insight to the people she met.

Everybody loves Jack when they meet him. He is a minister who likes to be called a preacher, but the truth of the matter is he is a minister, a life-giving minister. His manner is unique. He's not handsome and he does not appear to be a brilliant man. He does give off a quality of appreciation which is not often found today. Jack's offer to give life is best seen in the way he places his arm around a person's shoulder and says appropriately, "I love you." Jack does not offer this love indiscriminately for he understands affection is something many people need but cannot take. He is, however, able to sense the moment when people most need someone who cares. The gentle way in which he offers himself as one to lean upon has led him to be the rock to many people in time of trouble. Jack loves humor and uses it to cause people to let down their defenses with him. I do not know anyone who fears him. His plain manner has opened many doors to other people.

Life giving can be offered in many ways. Writing is one of these. Billie is a writer. She doesn't write about everything. She concentrates on saying something about life. Billie has keen insights into the predicament of twentieth century people. She speaks to these predicaments with hope. She is able to create within the minds of her readers not only a vision of the way things are, but a passion to make them like they ought to be. Listen to her words:

> Etched mockingly against a black backdrop of plenty are faces of need.
> The technological future, giving birth to lasers and air-conditioned space ships,
> Falls short of Utopia;
> To the hungry, the sick, the oppressed and the stranger, hope is still-born.

Writers who are life givers need people to contemplate the things they write. The words above should not be treated lightly or quickly but should be lived with and loved.

There's a life giver whose name I do not know. This person's message came on a card. It said, "Because there was us once, there can never be the same you or the same me again. It's not the touch of a fairy wand that changes things. It's the touch of passing people." A friend sent this card to remind me of an experience we once had, and in doing so caused that experience to live again. Often life givers need the words of other people to say what they need most to say. By the same token, the people of our perishing world need to be given the words of hope and life which some unknown writer sends by the way of a life giver.

Robert is dead. I wanted to cry when the news came, but the tears would not come. Robert was the doctor who diagnosed my wife's illness. I can still remember when he told me it was multiple sclerosis. He told my wife and me some of the things we might expect from this disease. We did not live much longer in the city where Robert practiced, but through the years we kept in touch. Many times he and his wife were a source of understanding and strength. I can recall one particular experience during a time when my wife was having a serious attack and hope for her life was very slim. I needed to talk to someone. Robert and Jean invited me to come to their home. I went and spent the night. During this time, I shared a lovely meal and some time with the children. During the evening Robert and I walked along a park-like area behind his home and talked. We shared the uncertainty of life and the certainty of death. We talked about the unpredictability of a disease and what it could do to a human being. Neither of us would have believed that evening that his death would come before my wife's, but it did. I carry within me forever the life which Robert shared with me that night. He is gone, but what he gave I plan to offer to many people whose circumstances need what he had to give.

Bob Williams cannot leave things alone. But that's how we find many problems being left. Alone. Bob sees many people in his life who are content to live with the dregs of life rather than with life's riches. They have settled down with things as they are. Problems are something to talk about to people but not things to solve. Tom is the kind of life giver who insists that every person with a problem take a new look at it. But he is there to help. Bob has found people could not solve their problems because they could not initiate action. This often grew out of their inability to make a decision. Bob's motto in life giving is "We will make something happen." And that's what he helps people do. Bob was trained in mathematics and is quite competent in thinking up ways to solve problems. Bob encourages people to make things happen, and he offers to be their partner in seeing that the right things happen in the right way. I have seen him work with parents who had difficulties with their children, with young women who had problems with their mothers-in-law, and mothers-in-law who had problems with their daughters-in-law. Bob doesn't care who he helps. He prefers to help those who have decided they have a problem which can't be helped.

Life giving, like love, is a many-splendored thing. It is the life giver who makes it so. People in their life giving are like the kaleidoscope with which I played as a child. Each one is beautifully different and intriguing to watch. As I remember many of the life givers I've known, I feel strong regret that only a chapter is being devoted to the stories of a few and numerous others must go unnoticed. All of them are ordinary people but extraordinary in what they do for others.

Jean means much to the lives of many people including my own. Her life giving is best understood in what she does. The phone rings and my wife picks up the receiver. Jean will invariably say, "I'm coming over," and she does. And when she comes it always makes a difference. Most often she brings something—flowers, cake, a picture. She gives not only of herself but a gift which also says "I care." I'm not sure how many years Jean has been coming to see my wife. Most people are willing to go see an invalid for awhile, but few have the capacity to go back again and again. They have

even less capacity to make their visits meaningful to the invalid.
It's very rare indeed when an invalid has one who comes over
the years and is looked for with eager anticipation. Life givers
are this kind, and Jean is a life giver. At the end of the day when
Jean has come my wife always tells me she's been there. She may
not describe what has happened or what they talked about, but
always she shows more life. And I know who gave it to her.

Thomas Eugen is a person who needs to help people. He has
his own company and has watched it grow under his own direction.
He has tried an extraordinary thing with the people who work
for him. Through the use of simple personality tests he has tried
to give each of his employees a better understanding of themselves.
In conversation with them and using information he has, he's been
able to help more than one give up the inadequate ways of living
they have been using for years. He has shared this experience with
me. More than half a dozen of these employees holding themselves
back or experiencing hurt because of undesirable behaviors they
had unconsciously established as habits. Tom learned how to iden-
tify the causes for these inadequacies. He has learned how to offer
insights to his employees. He is not a perfect life giver, but he
has done far more for these people than anyone else they have
ever met. Some have found brand new lives because of him. Others
are already making a better life for themselves and their families.
Life giving is a legitimate activity for people who direct and super-
vise the lives of others in business settings. In fact, one of the
greatest privileges any executive or manager will ever have is that
of using his vocation as a means of life giving. Tom is such a
manager. He is a life giver.

Life giving is a capacity we must develop. Regretfully it is not
something with which we are born. People become life givers during
their lifetime. Some are aware of the moment when they develop
this capacity. Others would be surprised to find that they have
it. One of the great joys of my life is to observe people as they

come to experience for the first time what it means to be a life giver. Many of these have shared with me their experiences.

Ruth is an attractive woman. People like to be around her. She is always being a helper to others, and in fact, has been a source of real strength as she has led many people to a better understanding of Christ and the Bible. She has through these years hidden from people the hurt she has personally known. Some time ago she determined to dispose of old emotional hurts. Now she has begun to help people in her family express themselves. She told me of an experience that happened one day with her young son. He had for too long manipulated his family to get a great deal of personal attention. He used a technique on his mother to accomplish this goal. She had perceived this behavior and warned him that he would no longer receive her protection from other family members. She extended her insights to other areas of relationship to this child. Through the years when she prepared to leave home, she would tell him that she was leaving and for him to come along. He paid little attention and would continue in his activity absorbed with what he was doing. He accepted no responsibility for himself. On one occasion she told her son that she was leaving in ten minutes. She did leave and he was shocked. He went on about his business, left the home, and came back later that day after his mother had returned. When he raised the question with her regarding her action of leaving him she dealt with his emotions. "It made you mad for me to do that, didn't it?" she asked. He responded immediately and confirmed with words and feelings that he had gotten quite mad. She accepted his anger and acknowledged that she had been unjust to him in the past but not on this occasion. She explained that her communications to him were quite clear, and where she had been unjust was in continuing to wait for him in years past when she had told him she was leaving. She warned him that the day of her being responsible *for* his behavior—his coming and his going—was over. She promised to be a just mother, helping him to be responsible for himself. His response was ready acceptance of the experience and the new way of relating. This life giver, a mother, was elated. So was I, for she had brought in these moments a new dimension, a new responsibility to the relationship between herself and her son.

Some weeks ago my phone rang late one night. Upon answering it, I heard the excited voice of a person whom I met first about ten years ago. I came to know him much better in some crisis experiences in his life some three years ago. He lives halfway across the country from me. He had experienced the thrill of life giving and felt he had to share with me. His words were, "Today I was a life giver."

"Tell me about it," I said.

He had just returned from a meeting where he had met a man who had a responsible position as a leader of people. The man had many competencies. He had been trained so that these competencies were almost overpowering. Approaching forty years of age, this man had never given attention to who he was or who he was going to be. He was carried along much like the debris in the rushing rain water. He was groping for meaning—how to see himself, how to see his work, how to see his life. These were the exact problems this friend of mine had faced several years before. He shared his own experience with this man who was almost a stranger. There was nothing radical in the way he did it nor what he had to say, but he simply shared what he had found about living life. He told of the life that had been given to him and the insights with which he was living. He told the results that had come to him from seeing himself as the son of his mother and father and also the son of God. He helped the man to understand how he had separated his father's and mother's strengths and the strengths that came to him from his Christian experience. He described the process of accepting those ways of thinking and feeling and doing which his parents had given him, based upon their adequacy. He also told how he had come to reject without remorse his parents' behavior where it was not adequate and where he had to live his own life. It worked. The man began to see. He began to describe what he wanted from life and what he expected to give life. As the time went by, the man who came to him lost went away having found life. Just as important my friend, the new life giver, had tasted the fruit of the life giver. He found it difficult to control his feelings of joy. I told him it was not necessary to control his positive feelings. Together we rejoiced for we knew that we had experienced something which most men never know.

Relatives, even mothers-in-law, can be life givers. My mother-in-law is. She is always doing things for people. I could describe how she helps small children or college students, but her life giving to me is the best example. A wife's condition as an invalid makes life difficult for a husband; a fact many people know from experience. The husband has to take over some mother activities with children, house management, and some social responsibilities. Not only does he have to get these done while looking after his regular responsibilities, but there are the additional matters related to the illness. Most men give up part of their life, usually recreation, in order to keep up. My mother-in-law keeps me playing golf. She knows I like and need it and that my best time to play is when it is most difficult to get someone to stay with my wife. She will give up any of her own plans to do this. Because of her life giving, I am a less tense, healthier person who is able to give more to others. In addition to this service, she gives freely in more ways than I can describe even if I used this whole book.

Frank had heard and discussed the concept of life giving. He liked to help people and did many things for people. He knew there had been occasions in his life when he was with people who needed a unique kind of help. At such times he was hesitant, even fearful that he was inadequate to help. He had developed the common human behavior of doing nothing if he was not certain he would succeed. Frank told me of his first experience in deliberately intervening when he experienced the feeling of fear. It happened with a colleague in the business where he worked. This person had in past years rejected religious belief as having no meaning to him. He had become a professional in his field of work and found in his work a lot of meaning for his life. It and the social experiences his wife and his family had seemed to satisfy him. That ceased to be true when his young son was accidentally killed. His inner world came apart. There were not enough resources within. It showed on his face. It could be heard in the tone of his voice. Although he worked in the midst of many, it was Frank who saw and heard. He reached out with the simple words, "I'm sorry," and to the deeper problem the man had. He asked where the source of this man's strength lay. Frank reminded him he had once known God and the promises of God to a hurting man. Frank challenged that person to rethink ideas about God and man which had been laid aside. He invited him to accept the prayers which my friend and his family were offering. He invited him to let someone else share his hurt. Frank asked that he be allowed to care for this man. It is no surprise to me that this man, though middle-aged, did not resist. He responded by accepting the life giver's offer. And, today, his life shows the difference. His adjustment to the death of his son is only a small part of the results. He is seeking now to be what was possible for him to be all these years. My friend, who now knows what it is to intervene deliberately, moves onward in his practice of life giving. One was not enough. Now there are others, and with each additional one there is a celebration—a celebration we share with one another.

Ordinary people, that is all we will ever be. Strangely enough, this is all the perishing people of our world really need. This is especially true if as ordinary people we recognize our capacity to be life givers, accept our possibilities for being instruments to others as they develop new ways of thinking, feeling, and acting. We are ordinary people who know that God has placed the Source of Life within.

SIX

Life Giving Is Exciting

Life giving is exciting. We get to know people. We share with people in the drama of their lives. We suffer with people in their failures. We celebrate with people in their achievements. That which we share becomes our own experience; the residue of this experience is the true quality of our life. So as we challenge each reader to engage actively with humanity in the great experience of life, we want to share some of the exciting times that have been ours with people.

Will Rogers, the famous American humorist, is often quoted as having said he never met a man he did not like. I wish I could say that. I can say I have never gotten to know a man whom I did not love. The truth is there are too many strangers in my world. What I find to be true of myself is also true of others. People are strangers in their own homes, with people they think are their close friends, and most especially at work where they spend most of their life. This may sound unbelievable to you. It has to many people whom I have challenged with the idea that the members of their family are strangers to one another. Some people who have worked close together for a quarter of a century and who feel they know one another find they have only scratched the surface. I have practiced helping people get to know people they felt they already knew. To understand or truly know a person we must know what has happened to him. This means listening with understanding as an individual tells about his life, his family, his hurts, and his joys. It has been interesting for me to discover the things children know about their parents. Most parents select unconsciously what they want their children to know. Very few children know the full life experience of their parents—especially those parents who have shielded children from knowing the undesirable experiences they've had and the hurt which such experiences have left with them. If we were to take the time to understand the events of a middle-aged person's life, what he thought about these events, what he felt about these events, it could consume several hours of time. Most parents have spent far more time than this talking about their life with their children, but they have done it in snatches of a few minutes at a time. Seldom have I met children whose parents have taken the time to tell their total life experience. Because of this, the children are living with strangers. I mean there is important information missing. What is true in this relationship is also true in the lack of understanding parents have for children. Because we see what is happening to our children does not mean we understand what is really going on with our children. Their emotional reactions and much of their thinking is kept inside. Quite often because of the press of activities, we parents do not take time to get our children to completely express themselves.

One might feel it is impossible to get to know people on this level. I do not accept this conclusion. It's a matter of caring and a matter of discipline. During the past years I've come to know hundreds of people at a level which they have not shared with others in their life; not because there were secrets to be kept, but simply because no one took the time.

In developing our understanding of people we need to realize the individual consists not just of what has happened to him but what he thinks about it and how he feels about it.

One of the extra benefits of getting to know a person is to become acquainted with his father, mother, brothers, sisters, and even grandparents. Some of these people are exceedingly colorful persons. It is exciting to think of some of the people whom I've never seen but come to know through their sons or grandsons. I have thrilled at the way people cope with unbelievable hardships that they experience in life. I can imagine the faces and bodies of many people whom I've never met but who have become very real to me as one of their descendants shared his life. One of these is a man whose son I know. His son is an artist and a manager. The home was one in which hardship was the way of life. It was a frontier home in the Midwest, and the father earned his livelihood as a mule skinner. The mother, on the other hand, was a sensitive and gentle person. As the son told the story of his family in picturesque language, he drew a picture of a stern father who was tough from working with mules and who used the language of the mule skinner. As he told this story those listening became aware of the great strengths which this man possessed. His son gained a new regard and appreciation for his father. The son came to see that his capacity to manage people was a gift to him from this mule skinner. Meeting this man's father was enjoyable. I wish that in life I might have known him. If I had ever met this man I would have listened to what he had experienced in life. I would like to know the hardships that drove him as a very young child to begin working with grown men. He would have told me how he learned to curse before he was twelve and curse in a respectable mule skinner fashion.

Once when a group of friends had spent almost a day listening to each other tell of their lives, we came to the time of departing. One of the persons expressed what I've heard many times over. "Oh for just a few more hours. This is so exciting!"

Getting to know people is exciting—especially when we take the time to understand them, to watch them laugh about experiences that have happened, to see tears stream from the eyes of men who have forgotten how to cry, to hear them tell of the angers, fears, and hopes they've known in their lives.

I recall one group of people whom I hoped would get to know each other better. Seven of them worked together. These people had known each other for at least eight years and some had been acquainted for twenty-five. When I told them they were working with strangers they laughed. I said nothing in response to their laughter. When the experience of sharing was over, I asked the group again, "Were you working with people you knew, or were you working with strangers?" Obviously, their answer was, "they were strangers." The point I'm making is that people do not know people just because they've lived with them for long periods of time. We don't really know people the way they are until we have listened at length to their life story. I challenge you to use your own family as a place to get to know people. I suggest that you, the reader, volunteer to be first to tell your family or close friends who you are.

Life is full of danger, conflict, and injustice. We need not cross town, go to a ghetto area, or travel to a far country to encounter these. They are ever present where we live daily. Sharing with people in the dramatic events of life is exciting. Unfortunately most people are unaware of the drama that is taking place in their own home and community. Or, if they are aware of this drama, feelings such as fear or anger cause them to overlook the true nature of what is happening.

We are becoming more aware today of the danger about us. For many decades Americans have been relatively free of external danger. Those who live in the urban areas of our nation are now being confronted with increased causes for fear. But there was, and always will be, dangers where people live. To assess the prevalence of danger in your community, assuming that you live in an urban area, try this mental game. Imagine a stake in your front yard or porch. To this stake is a rope one-quarter of a mile long. Taking the end of the rope in your hand, walk a circle around the stake. Do not be bothered by the obstacles that are in your way. When you have finished the circle and returned to the spot where you began, you will have encompassed a number of homes, apartments, or other dwellings and businesses where there are people. Try to think of the people in this area who are overusing drugs and alcohol, or actually acting out physical aggression upon other members of the family. Husbands and wives who are endangering their marriage. Children, youth and adults who are not being allowed to be themselves. How frequently are children hurt because of the rough terrain? Physical danger is to some degree within this area which you live.

These are but a few of the dangers which are inherent in the average setting in which we live. Each individual and family who shares in one of these experiences of danger is in need of a life giver. Perhaps that life giver should be in his home, but there is no guarantee that such will be the case. Our sensitivity to the hurt that is present when people face danger or live with the results of dangerous experiences alerts the life giver to an opportunity of sharing.

I have lived in my residence for almost fifteen years. It is on a street that is not a thoroughfare. The speed limit is thirty miles an hour. The road does give access to a number of areas within our community and a fair amount of traffic passes upon it. Adjacent to my lot is a bridge spanning a small creek. The creek is approximately eight feet below the level of the road bed. The bridge is at the low point of the road from both directions, and forms a hollow. If an automobile travels too fast, it will receive a slight lift as it passes over the bridge. During the years I have lived in my home, there have been five cases of persons, who driving too fast, approached the bridge, lost control of the car, and ended up either in the creek or nearby. By the sounds that are made I can tell when an automobile is going to wreck. On several late night occasions I have been able to leave my bed, go through my house to the back door, and be halfway to the bridge before the automobile came to a full stop. Most of the time the help

I have given has been to the occupants of the car or to people who have gathered. The dramatic aspect of these experiences are burned into my memory. Less clear to me are the people who were involved or the people who came to watch. I do remember on more than one occasion holding a person who was injured until the ambulance arrived. I have also helped to remove people from their danger. On occasions I have offered comfort to an uninjured person who was in the car. In all of these cases I have not done enough because when people are in immediate danger and the damage that it does, they are limited in the help they can receive.

The same kind of situation obtains when damage is being done within the home setting through drugs and alcohol or by dominating personalities and violent people. It takes time to give help and sometimes circumstances do not permit this time. Fortunately there are many dangerous events that allow time for intervention. Child beating or wife beating are behaviors that do not come and go in one day. The same is generally true of alcoholism and drugs. The environment in which such events occur is unhealthy, and this unhealthy environment takes time to develop and time to dissipate. All of us are neighbors to people who live in a great deal of danger. In fact, there may be people in your own household who live in continual danger. The excitement that the life giver finds in committing himself to such people is not itself a worthy value to motivate one to life giving, but the excitement in such cases should make us aware of the significance of what is involved if we do not act.

As dangers are found in our homes and community, so is injustice. Many injustices are subtle. But all injustices are dramatic and create conflict. The conflict created by injustice either remains in the person to whom the injustice was done or is brought out into the open. The successful resolution of injustice is an area in which life givers could spend the rest of their time. Injustice occurs frequently even in the best of homes. It was for this reason that the words "I'm sorry" were created. I cannot agree with the movie expression that love is not having to say you're sorry. In fact, it's the people who have the capacity to love that can say, "I'm sorry." When there is no love there appears to be no healthy capacity to say these words.

An injustice would not be so bad and perhaps not so exciting if having been done it could be put aside and forgotten. The human personality has a way of accumulating feelings that occur when injustice is done. Unless an injustice is righted or an effort is made to right it, individuals accumulate angers beyond their control. Accumulated angers become hatreds that express themselves in more violent fashion than is healthy. Earlier we said many people have not learned the nature of emotions and for what they are to be used. Anger is the feeling God gave to us to warn that an injustice is being done to us or may be being done to us. The feeling of anger leaves to the reasoning part of our minds the determination of whether it is a real or an imagined injustice. Anger leaves to the reasoning part of our mind to determine what response shall be made. If, however, our reasoning mind does not act responsibly toward the feelings of anger, then these feelings will accumulate until they become hatreds. Or if the reasoning mind does an inadequate job, these emotions of anger may be expressed in an undisciplined and violent manner. This is why unsolved injustice is perhaps the greatest source of unhealth and evil in our world today. Injustice is dramatic and always exciting because so much emotion is triggered. Watching an injustice occur even between children is extremely interesting.

I saw a child who was attending a nursery school being bitten by another child in this school. The workers immediately separated the children, took the bitten child and tried to comfort him. They were uncertain how to care for the child who was doing the biting. They did not understand the behavior adequately and knew only that they must restrain his behavior. It was not the first time this had happened. It appeared to me that it might not be the last time it would happen. To be bitten is an injustice, not to have this injustice righted is an even greater injustice. When we see the atmosphere where such behavior takes place change from that of happy playing children to one of fear and anxiety, not only for the two children involved but for all the children and adults within the setting, we sense what injustice does to life.

A classic picture of injustice, which it was intended to be, is seen in the story of Brer Rabbit and Tar Baby. You will recall that Brer Fox intended to make his lunch of Brer Rabbit. Being a sly insightful fox he knew the outgoing nature of Brer Rabbit. He had observed Brer Rabbit's need to get attention from others. He knew Brer Rabbit's difficulty when people failed to give him this attention. When Brer Fox constructed Tar Baby, he did so for a purpose.

That morning Brer Rabbit came down the road and spied Tar Baby. Brer Rabbit was just being himself . . . friendly, outgoing, and interested in others. He believed in justice for all men (and rabbits). He spoke to Tar Baby as is the custom for one human being to do to another. Tar Baby's failure to respond was at the very least an impolite human behavior. When Tar Baby continued silence in response to Brer Rabbit's efforts to greet him, his behavior had to be characterized as rude. When in due time Brer Rabbit concluded an injustice was being done, he based it on the fact that anybody that looks like a human being ought to act like a human being. This is a fair premise, but not one that we can always use in relating to people or tar babies. Brer Rabbit did not stop to reason that Tar Baby might not really be a human capable of human responses. Instead, his emotions did what they're supposed to do. Anger said to him, "an injustice is being done to you by this tar baby, are you going to take it?" Brer Rabbit without a great deal of reasoning turned to the use of threat, and having made his threat found it necessary to carry it out, which, as a courageous rabbit he did. We're all acquainted with the fact that within a matter of moments Brer Rabbit was all stuck up in Tar Baby. This is where injustice leads. We have all met people like Brer Fox, Brer Rabbit, and Tar Baby. They're all around us. In fact, we ourselves are like them at times.

The story of Brer Rabbit and the Tar Baby has excited children for years. I find that even adults get excited when they see the real plot that was taking place. But this fiction is not nearly as dramatic as the real life situations of a life giver. They are like adventures in every sense of the word.

One of these was the drama between a father and daughter. I think of this experience in terms of a title called "The Subject Is Physics." The father and daughter were in conflict. The daughter was having some difficulty being just the person she wanted to be. She felt crowded in her attempts because of the over-direction her father was seeking to provide. He felt he knew what was best for her—not only in school work but in a number of other areas of her life. Since she did not feel adequate to cope with him in the several areas of conflict, she chose one—the subject was physics. This was his choice, a field in which he excelled and in which she had the capacity to excel. She knew that she could pass this course, but her attitude toward it was hostile and antagonistic. She made physics the battle ground on which she fought her father. Her grades were not up to the standard of which she was capable. When father, daughter, and I shared this experience, we came to see that the conflict over physics actually was the daughter trying to say, "I want to be me, I don't want to be you, Dad. I want to be the girl that I am. I want to become the woman that I want to become." This young lady has worked through her problems with her father. She might have forgotten a lesser experience than this, but it remains a symbol to her of the injustice she felt was being done. It was a thrill to share this drama with this father and daughter. Three persons are the richer for it.

Life giving is suffering with people in their failures. All of us have known the experience of failure. Many know failure in its simplest form, but others have known the depth of failure—what it means for their entire life to be taken away. They know what it means to start anew, to try again. People who have experienced failure know also what it is to hurt. Hurting itself is not bad. Hurting tells a person, and those around, of the suffering that is taking place within a personality. But hurting people do need attention. Too often at a moment when an individual is experiencing failure and consequently hurt, they must do it alone or only with the help of a wife, husband, or children. Life givers are alert to people who are experiencing failures and are prepared to give attention to their hurts. The methods of the life giver to the hurting person include reassurance and affection.

Oftentimes a failure in performance leads a person to believe that he is no good. This feeling of inadequacy is a dreadful thing to experience. I have met people who were incompetent in the job they were doing. On the other hand, I know very few people who are incompetent persons. We need to separate successful achievement in roles or jobs which we do from the achievement of being a person. The life giver does this. He helps the individual to assess himself, first discovering anew the person who is within and helping the individual to recognize the strengths that he has. Furthermore, the life giver helps him to analyze why he failed or thinks he failed. The life giver seeks to help the person accept his failure as a temporary experience, one that can be offset by new achievements in the same or other fields. He challenges the person who has failed to consider whether he has tried to perform in an area he should not have entered. He does not conclude for the person whether it was a mistake or not.

Most of all, the life giver offers to that person who has failed his warm affection and appreciation. Failure is an experience of loneliness. There is no way to keep it from being so, but there is a way by which we can soften the harshness of this loneliness. In failure, an individual must plumb his own depths and discover reality. The life giver can stand beside him and let him know nearness, personal appreciation, and affection.

Have you ever watched an athletic event where a person poorly trained for losing failed? Often as friends try to offer condolence, such persons jerk away and pull off to themselves. This is not an uncommon human behavior for this is an expression that failure brings on. Restored relationships within a community where one has failed leads to a quicker readjustment. Achievement comes easier and self-esteem is redeemed. The life giver knows the excitement of restoring esteem to the heart of a person suffering from failure.

Jim was a competent and well-educated young man. He was employed by a large company in the business end of its operation. Soon the leadership of the company discovered his capabilities. In a matter of four years he had moved by promotion to the fourth job. Everyone was proud of Jim. They applauded his achievements. There was little jealousy on the part of anyone. Jim had tried four jobs, each of them in an area different from the one before. Again his last job was an assignment which called for him to function in a fashion new to him. A year went by and he had some success. But he also had a number of problems. Another year passed and there was dissatisfaction in the way he performed the job. The time came when those who were responsible for Jim had to confront him with his lack of capacity in the latest job. They offered him opportunities to work in other places. They could not, at the time, provide him equal remuneration. Jim, who had succeeded all the years of his life was less concerned with pay than he was over the fact that he could fail. His embarrassment and loss of self-esteem could easily be seen in his attitude and physical appearance. He was so trained to reject failure that when it happened to him, he found he was rejecting all of himself. He became undisciplined in the things he said and did, and in due time found it necessary to leave the company where he was employed. I remember talking to him. He could not understand nor believe what had happened. He did believe it was not his fault and at the same time he expressed the feeling he was no good anymore. Over the weeks we talked about the way he felt and thought. Gradually healthy feelings flowed back within him. He came to accept himself again as a person of value who had meaning to other people. I spoke of what he had both meant to me and done for me in months past, and pointed out that it was impossible for him to take away from our relationship these values. Together we explored new possibilities for him vocationally. He saw that he had certain strengths in areas where he would have great difficulty failing. He began to seek employment and found it. Today Jim is located in a position of equal status and pay to the one he left behind. He has successfully passed through an experience of failure. He looks with eagerness and anticipation to a long and fruitful life in his new vocation. But he knows what it is like to fail He knows the feelings of failure. He is now prepared to face the little and big failures that will come to his life and to help others with whom he lives face the failures that will come to them.

Life giving is not always relating to people in their miseries and tragedies. Life giving is celebrating with people their achievements. Success does not come every day of one's life. In fact, success comes so infrequently that celebration, for most people, is in order. I spoke earlier about the difficulty most Americans have in adjusting to prosperity. There seems to be a similar handicap when it comes to people celebrating. Think of the celebrations your own family has had in the past months. How many parties, banquets, or other festivities have been held to celebrate achievements? Life and success ought to be enjoyed. Celebrations are special periods of enjoyment. I'm always grateful when I am invited to be a part of someone's celebration. I'm always glad when I have an opportunity to express to another person that I am aware he has made some contribution or received some worthy recognition.

Think of the things that are taking place around us which give the life giver an opportunity to respond. Just in the past months I've heard people say to me things like this, "I'm getting married." "I'm going to graduate in June." "I'm retiring next month." "I've got a new job." "I'm going to be on the team." "We have a new home!" "I joined the church last Sunday." "Our team won the state championship!" These are only a few of the remarks which we can hear almost any week from people who have felt the exhilaration of success. What a marvelous opportunity for us to add to their feelings of success our own appreciation for them as contributing persons to our society and community.

There are many people in our world who no longer taste the sweetness of achievement. Their environment has done its damage. They have been pushed either down or out. They feel rejected and unwanted. Some of these are young people not yet in grade school. Others are children. Great hosts of them are senior citizens who have passed the stage of performing productively for their society. The life giver is one who interprets achievement according to an individual's capacity to succeed rather than in terms of society. This means that the life giver celebrates with another person many times when the newspaper or the community is unaware of the achievement.

I have a habit I know some people think is silly. It may be, but I'm not yet ready to give it up. I like to applaud people for doing things that represent their own achievements. It is not unusual for us to applaud entertainers, people who give speeches, people who are graduating or retiring. But the person who is just doing well what he's supposed to do is often left without applause. Sometimes I clap my hands over a good job one or several of my employees has done. Can you imagine how people must feel about being applauded for turning in a report. Why not? And thus far I've never had any to tell me not to do so. In my pastoral counseling, when people have done an especially fine task of trying on a new behavior or a new feeling, I clap with applause to show them that I am aware of their achievement. Silly but meaningful to someone with whom I am celebrating an achievement. Life giving may be accomplished with behaviors as simple as applause or a few words of sincere appreciation.

One of the reasons, I believe, adults grow less and achieve less in new fields than youth is directly related to the matter of expressing appreciation for achievements. Consider the small child two and three years of age who is learning at the most rapid rate he will ever learn in his life. How often have we seen parents hover over these children encouraging a new step, a new word, or some other new behavior? Think of the excitement around the house when the baby takes its first step, has its first tooth, says its first word, reads its first word, and forms its first sentence. What sixty or seventy-year-old adult has been given this much attention this many times in the last year? Motivation to become, motivation to grow, motivation to live the abundant life is partially found in the acceptance of our contributions by significant persons in our community. Life givers are significant persons. Life givers acknowledge contributions others are making.

Some life givers are models of living. Mary and I have been married for more than twenty years. Much more than half this time she has struggled and suffered from multiple sclerosis. She no longer walks and now has difficulty using her hands. Extreme fatigue is her constant companion. Yet she has never given up. When I travel, old friends ask how she is. I reply, "Mary never misses Sunday church, a wedding, or a party." How does she do it? Why does she do it? It's her way of being a life giver. Unbelievable numbers of people tell her and me how her struggle gives them courage and determination to press on during difficult life circumstances. Some life givers are models of living. They don't write, talk, or touch. They just climb impossible mountains and in doing so say to the rest of us, "You can, too!"

Life giving provides an opportunity for the life giver to use all of his mind, emotions, and energy. This is why life giving is so exciting. It is total participation. The life giver keeps his senses alert to what is really taking place. He opens his emotions to experience the full range of feelings. He produces energy and uses it in order to be to other people what they need. Excitement is a healthy emotional state. It produces energy and creates anticipation and expectancy within a person.

SEVEN

Count On It Hurting

Fire flashed from his eyes! Flushed cheeks and agitated movements signaled his anger. "What do you think you're doing!!" he shouted at me! The situation was confirmed. Somebody didn't like me or what I had done.

"Her husband is going to whip you," the man continued. He had me scared for I don't like someone beating me up. In fact, I began to fear that this enormous man who was shouting at me might decide to do the beating. I tensed myself for an attack and put forth a question, "Who is going to whip me and why?" He responded with far more than I requested. Somehow a misunderstanding between a man and his wife had occurred. She had sought my help. The husband felt I had told his wife what to do. He blamed me for their predicament. I became the target of his anger. I hurt for hours. I could feel fear in my stomach for hours. My whole body ached with frustration and hopelessness.

I wish I could get beyond the point of hurting when someone's anger, frustration, or suspicion is directed to me. I can't. Hurt is not avoided even though the efforts are intended to help—to give life. In life giving one can get hurt. Because life giving love is not careful, the life giver can expect to know a lot of hurt. He comes to count on it.

Life giving at this point is much like football or other contact sports. I asked a friend of mine who played college and pro football why he kept on taking the severe physical punishment which had included broken bones and knee operations. "I love the game," he replied. It is for this same reason a life giver will continue to expose himself to hurt. He loves to help people.

A life giver must learn to expect hurt for it comes in many ways. Very seldom is he actually hurt physically but frequently he will experience emotional pain. His pain may result from rejection, displaced anger, compassion, or failure. If effective he will know hurt from all of these.

Many people cannot and will not take help that is offered. This is their right. To try to make a person take help he does not want is wrong. It violates the whole spirit of life giving. But what of situations where the actions of a person is destroying the relationship with a spouse, family, or co-workers. What does a life giver do? If he cares he keeps trying to get such a person to accept help. Rejection is a common response when an effort is made. "Leave me alone," "Get away from me," "You're a dirty ______" are just a few verbal expressions of rejection. Put feeling and physical action with them and imagine things that happen.

Rejection hurts. It stirs the feelings of loneliness. Each time rejection comes one senses the curse of human life: no person will ever be able to escape the reality of his individuality and aloneness. Most of us avoid our loneliness. We have many techniques for doing so and often succeed for long periods of time. This comes to an abrupt end when we experience rejection. What is happening to me? How can he misunderstand me so? Why would anyone not like me? These rational thoughts are often the reflections of a personality in pain. The words ought to be; I hurt and I ache.

Rejection provokes the feeling of fear. Hidden within all of us is an active or latent feeling that we are inadequate. Each new experience of rejection awakes the feeling to do its damage to our adequate and confident self. The question "What's wrong with me?" haunts us. Fear that we may be what another thinks churns our emotions. After an experience of rejection, hours or days may pass before we are again at peace with ourself.

Marshall was an alcoholic. He had been for almost six years. His wife and three children suffered the consequences of his alcoholism. By the time a friend and I became interested in this family, Marshall had begun regularly to beat his wife and children. The day we first went to see Marshall he was as sober as he ever got. But he was as antisocial as anyone I've ever met. As soon as he discovered our purpose he started to curse and threaten. An hour of continuous abuse drained our energy and convinced us we were unwanted and completely unappreciated. We left. I hurt all night. For days when I would recall things this man said I would get upset. In one hour he had shaken my whole being. He reminded me of what I already knew. Sometimes it hurts to help.

A life giver is sometimes hurt by the spillover of a person's anger or hate for someone else. Usually the anger or hate is given because the attacker trusts the life giver to take it because no one else will do so. And the life giver may, but not without experiencing the accompanying hurts. Such expressions always leave me with emotional bruises. What is an emotional bruise? Like sore and blue places from being pushed or grabbed roughly, they accumulate without our awareness but leave us uncomfortable and overly sensitive where they exist. A bruised ego may suffer in a physical form. A tired body that doesn't respond to one's command quickly may be the result of emotional bruises. Disappointment or slight depression are feelings that sometimes come when people direct anger to us that should have been given to another.

A young friend of mine felt she had been done an injustice at her work. She came to me for help. I gave what I could. Her problem was bigger than my help and her ability. It dragged along.

I tried to provide encouragement where I could not assist in a satisfactory solution. The young lady felt I should do more and do it now. I did not feel this was best. She unloaded on me the anger toward her company and me. A three page letter started like this.

"Since you aren't going to listen to anything I have to say, I thought I would write it. Maybe it will not waste as much of your valuable time as a phone call would."

I knew who should have gotten most of this *put down* but these sentences and the rest of the letter stung sharply. I wanted to quit helping her. I wanted to look after my own hurt that came out of an effort to help. It is strange that a three page letter can tire and depress a person. But I know that it can.

The sensitivity that makes one care about another person in his predicament makes us vulnerable to suffering. Compassion is the kind of hurt that comes from sharing another person's life. It is feeling the hurt the other is feeling perhaps even when he does not feel it. When some people allow us to look at the tragedy that has come to them in life, we see the unbelievable damage evil can do. As long as I have been offering help to people I have never gotten beyond hurting when told about unusual damage being done to human life.

Jesus looked at the miserable life being lived by the inhabitants of Jerusalem. He knew the fear, hopelessness, depression, and anxiety that filled the city. He wept with compassion over the condition of these people—his people. He knew most of them would remain this way as would generations of descendants to follow. His words reflect his sorrow and suffering over their unnecessary way of life.

> O Jerusalem! You kill the prophets and stone the messengers
> God has sent you! How many times have I wanted to put my arms

around all your people, just as a hen gathers her chicks under her wings, but you would not let me! (Matthew 23:37-38)

The life giver may toss in his sleep, cry inside, or find tears in his eyes if he offers to help some people. The compassionate suffering of the life giver hurts. He *feels* his identity with all men. He feels that his destiny is the destiny of all men. He consciously or subconsciously feels that until human suffering is erased it will come again to strike him, his family, or some future descendant bearing his name. It is a hopeless feeling that some people experience all of their life. It is an undesirable feeling which the life giver will experience on occasion.

A young woman told of her experience in the home where the father was alcoholic. She described vividly what it was like when he was quite drunk. His morose condition led him to unbelievable aggression against this woman and younger children in the family. They were often beaten and threatened verbally. The situation was so bad that this young woman had to protect herself and her brothers and sisters. When they heard the father come home drunk at night they would slip out the back of the house and hide among trees and large boulders several hundred yards from the house. They remained there until the father would fall into a stupor. Sometimes the small children were kept out of the house and their beds until one or two a.m.

This is not the most brutal experience to which I have known people to be subjected, but when this young woman described her experience I, and others, suffered with her. I was not ashamed of the tears that came. I still suffer when the memory of her early life comes to my consciousness. I hurt with the unanswered question of why some life giving adult was not there to intervene. I feel shame, and the embarrassment from this shame, because so many of us adults are immobilized in responding to such situations. Is it because we are afraid to hurt?

Failure is a common thing. Yet most of us never learn to fail without a subsequent negative emotional experience. These are like mini nervous breakdowns. We come apart. Some are able to recuperate in a few minutes, others in a few hours, and some require days. Life givers experience a lot of failure in their efforts to offer help. These failures may result from a person's inability to receive help. It may come from the life givers inadequacy. Inadequacy or imperfection is the constant companion of the life giver. He never becomes good enough to cope with the problems of all men or all the problems of any man. But when a life giver sees magnificent possibilities slip away from a person and realizes he was actively intervening, he knows the hurt of failure.

The feelings that follow failure are many. They form a complex mixture that eats at one's insides. Small failures do slight damage. Important failures can hurt awfully bad. Mix up a potion of shame, embarrassment, chagrin, frustration, and fear. This, even in small amounts, can gnaw at healthy persons until there is pain. Scars from earlier failure may add to the hurt. A life giver friend of mine described his experience.

My friend was working with a young married couple who was having serious conflict. The wife had already brought up the idea of divorce when my friend's offer to help was accepted. The life giver enlisted the help of a minister, community social service agents, and a friend who had successfully solved a similar problem. The young couple participated in sessions to solve the problem. The husband was more receptive and adaptive than his wife. The effort lasted two months with many hours devoted by my friend. One night the marriage disintegrated with the departure of the young wife. I watched as my life giving friend suffered through her failure. She had ample inner resources to cope with her hurt, but the hurt was deep. It was several days before she felt herself— free to try again. She told me later she thought of how she should tend to her own business. She scolded herself for not acting sooner, for not getting the best help, and not using the right methods. As time passed and the hurt subsided, these criticisms of herself also subsided. Soon she was offering help again knowing that in doing so she could count on it to hurt.

People who want to help others have often asked me, "How can you avoid hurt when life giving?" I always answer, "You can't!" Hurt is part of the price one pays. It will always be so. However, one can do something about it.

Hurt is easier to bear if one does not accumulate it. Therefore, each time one feels a hurt occur, he must give attention until it has been made easy. This doesn't mean a life giver goes around cleaning up each tiny hurt minute-by-minute or by the hour. He simply stays alert to the nature of a hurt and brings this to his consciousness. The degree of pain should determine how quickly he lets the hurt get his best attention. I have known of life givers who stopped in the middle of life giving to attend their own hurt. This can be the right thing to do. It is if they are so distracted from their life giving to be of little or no effect.

The life giver must learn to care for his own hurts. This may require solitude to think and pray, rest in the form of sleep and play, or even the physical or spiritual comfort that comes from a trusted friend. Thinking is extremely therapeutic when the ego is hurting. Contemplating the fact of one's own worth and the temporary nature of hurt gives hope. Prayer provides a person contact with resources unique from those other men give. Prayer is my reminder that all does not depend upon me.

Many friends of mine have discovered how to sleep and play for the best good of the mind and body. Sleeping can be done for an hour instead of eight; at noon instead of night. Hurt can be reduced by relaxing the muscular and nervous system through sleep. Play does much the same. Some of my friends cook for play; others grow flowers; still others play chess or golf. The disciplined involvement of our neuro-muscular system in such activities helps to drain off the excessive amount of energy that the tense and hurting person produces.

Hurt can be decreased or diluted by sharing it. This is true of every feeling a person experiences. My daughter and wife love to share the hurt of their aching limbs with me. They do so by getting a gentle massage. I have done the same. Some people may wish to talk their hurt out. Sitting silently with another may be all some people need.

Whatever the method, the life giver must care for his hurts. He will not excel in offering help to others until he has learned to receive help for himself from others. Keeping hurts that may cause one to neglect or refuse to act deliberately is a luxury a life giver cannot afford and the world of people cannot survive. So if you give, count on it to hurt, then take care of your hurts.

EIGHT

Love Is Never Careful

Love is a relationship to another person. It is a relationship of commitment. The quality of one's love is determined by the strength of the commitment which the person has for the other. Some people speak of their love for humanity yet will not give a thirsty stranger water to drink. They will not ride a mile out of their way to meet the need of a neighbor. On the other hand, there are scores of people who go to the end of their life bearing burdens and hoping for a solution to the problems of a loved one. There are people who are up all night with the sick in their homes or with a child who is struggling with a problem.

Jesus said the greatest commitment that a man could have for another person is that of giving his life for that other person. We may be inclined to judge this as being able to give their life in death for another because Jesus certainly referred to his own act of giving his life in death for his friends. However, there is the matter of giving one's living life for a friend. In fact, love is giving of one's life. In the same sense a life giver has nothing other to offer than his own life to another. I have often heard children say about their father, "I don't want the **things** he can give me, I wish he would give me **himself.**"

I wish it were possible to say that giving one's self is what everyone can do because everyone has himself. But this is not true. One reason many people cannot give their life to others is because they do not have it. They have lost it. This, I think, is what Christ meant when he said whoever loves his own life will lose it; (John 12:25). I think Jesus is saying that whoever loves the style of life in which he grew up and wants to keep it more than to become himself and to be to his fellow man what God intended him to be will lose even the life style he wants to keep. This is the reason I described earlier the situation with Jesus and the rich young ruler. The young ruler's problem was his life style. He loved it better than the way he would live if he gave away his money and followed in the life style Jesus would give him. When we're trying to hold onto our own way of thinking, our own way of feeling, our own way of acting, we're bound to run into difficulties with people everywhere.

Love or commitment begins with one's self. We cannot love others if we do not love ourselves. This is what Jesus taught when he said, "Love thy neighbor as thyself." This saying is very much like a mathematical equation. It can be turned around at the word "as." Love thyself as thy neighbor. It is an equality of commitment that Jesus asked us to have. It is a commitment to our neighbor equal to the commitment we have to ourself and a commitment to ourself equal to that we have for our neighbor. This sounds not only like love but justice. If a man can be true to himself, he will be true to others. Shakespeare was correct when he wrote in his play, "To thine own self be true and it follows as the night follows the day thou canst not be false to any man."

This conclusion may create a mental dilemma in light of the fact that we quoted Scripture which says the person who loves his own life will lose it and also says "love thy neighbor as thyself." How can we resolve this apparent conflict? The person who must live whatever the price for living is in trouble. There are some things worth more than life itself. I believe Jesus is speaking to this.

Several things are worth more to me than life. At the top of this list I have to put the freedom to love. I have seen the destruction and death that unlove or hate brings. I have seen life that was more miserable to live than death. If some person could take away my freedom to love, I would have to fight to the point of losing my life to keep this necessary part of me. I also believe I would rather die than to give up my freedom to be me. I've seen many people who are more like robots under the direction of their parent, spouse, boss, or peers. Death is a better state than that of a machine. I would rather lose my life than lose a climate and environment in which I can be open and honest with myself and friends. When men must live in an environment which will not permit openness and honesty, then they might as well stop living for there will be no life of quality.

Fortunately, most readers of this book live in a society in which they are not being openly threatened in the practice of the above freedoms. There are, however, open and subtle enemies to the expression of these freedoms. The life giver soon becomes aware of these enemies and their threats to what he is seeking to accomplish. It is at this time he must evaluate the quality of his love including the degree of commitment he has to humanity, particularly to humanity which is in trouble. Since the question of openness and honesty is generally found in a limited problem area, it is easier for the life giver to determine whether he will challenge.

For this reason I have come to believe life giving love is never careful. This does not mean the loving person does not use reason, does not weigh circumstances, or does not use patience. It means commitment or love cannot afford to be careful. Love must exist; it must come into being. If the situation or circumstances surrounding involvement would deny or destroy this commitment, the life giver must not stop to count the cost.

I remember the first time I felt it was wise for a teen-ager to engage in open conflict with his father. This young fellow had for several years sought to live his own life and become the person he wanted to be while at the same time trying to please his father. The second was impossible to do as long as the young man insisted on doing anything other than what his father told him. He had been sent to me by a mutual friend who knew the boy's family. They were a respectable family, held in high esteem by everyone in the community. The young man was failing in his school work. He was drinking a lot and he was in the process of destroying his life. In listening to him I discovered he was not being allowed to be himself. Quite often people have asked me how can I say that since the youth was engaged in doing what it appeared he wanted to do. It was not difficult to discover, as the young man and I talked, that his failure in school was due to his inability to concentrate. His use of alcohol was an effort to reduce his anxiety, and his consideration of suicide was due to the feeling that he was a person of no value. All of these grew off of the unsatisfactory relationship he had with his father.

After we had spent some time together I expressed to him my feeling that he must learn to challenge his father openly, and he must learn how to do so in such a way that he did not lose in the conflict that was created. This youth immediately expressed fear that his father would not let him do this in the first place and that if he did, his father would "lower the boom." I pressed the matter and questioned if whether this was a time to be careful, for carefulness had been used too long to no avail. The conflict was already present, I pointed out to the youth, and that all he would be doing was to bring it into the open. We observed how a successful resolution of the conflict could prove to be a success not only for him but for his father. We discussed how a son can challenge a father. In this particular relationship we concluded that it was best for the youth to talk to his father in my presence. This approach might jeopardize my own relationship to the father because I would probably have to support the son in some of the positions that he was going to take. But, there seemed no better way. So we followed this route.

The father joined us and we began discussing the inadequate behavior his son had. The youth acknowledged how unsatisfactory it was to him and that he was really tired of the way he was living. He expressed how tired he was of the way he and his father were relating to one another. The father began immediately to describe the kind of behavior he would have to see in the son in order to relate to him.

At this moment I asked the father what he was trying to do to the son, what he was trying to make him. I asked the father if he wanted a puppet for a son or if he desired a person who could learn to be responsible for his own life. We pursued this idea by questioning whether the son should be directing his activities from within and directing these activities on the basis of a sound value system. The father agreed he would prefer the son to be responsible. The three of us looked at the father's behavior which for some time had not permitted or accepted failure on the part of his son. We observed how the father's own fear and anxiety over being a successful father became a hindrance to letting the son try certain ways of acting. We looked at the damage that had accumulated in the son due to this unwillingness on the father's part. We discussed the injustice that is involved in denying a person the right to be. Since the father was a religious person, I discussed the parable of the prodigal son, and its meaning in his own family situation. The son and father then discussed several incidences when the son had tried unsuccessfully to challenge his father. They discussed with one another the circumstances and how the father would not listen. The son described an occasion where he finally decided he would not try to discuss his life or his relationship to his father again.

In my presence he expressed anger toward his father saying his father appeared not to care what happened to him but only wanted to have his own way. The father and he engaged in some heated conversation. They said some things that had needed to be said months before. They continued to talk to one another. I served primarily to make certain each listened fairly to the other and understood what was being said. Over a matter of weeks these people learned to talk about subjects on which they did not agree. They learned to express anger when one or the other was being unfair. The father came to accept the fact that his son could challenge his ideas or his way of doing things and still love him. I am glad life giving love is not so careful but will challenge people who appear to like their destructive behavior and who give off signals that one will have to fight to make them switch.

A friend told me of her father who had to be true to himself. A middle-aged man who had worked for a manufacturing company most of his adult life, he was now its manager. Management was considering doing some things according to new ways. These did not appear to be fair and just to the employees who reported to this man. He took issue with the rest of the management. They did not accept his position but he remained determined. In due time it became a question of whether or not he would continue working in this position. He did consider the issue: who he was and who he could be. He loved to manage and had done a very excellent job, but the issue of integrity was too great. He resigned. He looked for his next self. He discovered he could use another of his talents for he was skilled in art. He offered this skill to the community in several commercial forms. They responded. They loved his service. He loved himself. He became successful again as he used creatively his whole being reserving nothing to continue a conflict he had brought to the surface and, without caution, resolved.

Scott and Sarah had dated their last two years of college. Now they were getting married. They were looking for an apartment when Sarah's mother offered to provide the money to allow them to live in an apartment nicer than Scott's income would provide. Scott was hesitant, but after listening to Sarah's pleas finally agreed. After the wedding, Sarah's mother offered her services in helping to furnish and decorate the apartment. She and Sarah had a great time together. They went shopping together several times a week. New things were added to the apartment regularly. Scott paid for some, but quite a few were added out of the graciousness of his mother-in-law. She was having a great time, almost as if she were the newlywed.

Soon Sarah's mother began to suggest how the house should be arranged, what colors ought to be used, and what should be purchased next. She and Sarah did not always agree, but Sarah could not defend herself. She found her mother controlling the way her apartment looked.

She tried to bring her conflict into the open. She could not. Then she began to be depressed. She would cry when Scott came home. She stopped enjoying doing things. Sleep was difficult to come. Scott decided to act.

He talked with me about his plan. He intended to confront his mother-in-law with what she was doing and the effect it was having upon Sarah and upon his own relationship to both families. He decided to discuss his approach with his father-in-law first and to tell him of Sarah's condition. Scott reviewed the possible reactions of his in-laws. He knew they might feel he was ungrateful or accuse him of immaturity. His love for Sarah far outweighed the disadvantages of leaving things as they were.

Scott met with his father-in-law and got his support. Together they went to Sarah's mother. Scott presented his problem. The mother was defensive. Then she began to cry. Scott was patient but persistent. He expressed an understanding that she meant no harm. He showed affectionate confidence that she could change her behavior. The mother-in-law began to respond to Scott's efforts.

She expressed again her real desire for Sarah's happiness. She acknowledged her over-eagerness might have caused the problem. She was willing to take a look at her behavior. There came a commitment from Scott's mother-in-law that with his help and the help of the father-in-law she would alter her behavior. Scott accepted her commitment and promised that he would see to it that her daughter enjoyed an exceedingly fine life.

Later Scott told Sarah what he had done and on another night both families got together and discussed the matter anew. For the first time in a long time Sarah was able to tell her mother the feelings that she had, the depression that had begun to come upon her and the hopelessness with which she looked toward her future with Scott. She expressed how she had long before realized that she was treating him unfairly and that she expected him to bear what she was unable to give to her mother. She apologized for this behavior and asked each of the people present to support her in a better behavior. From that second meeting, the families grew farther apart in their daily activities but closer together in their respect and trust for one another. A number of years have passed since this crisis occurred. Now Scott and Sarah have three children. They are settled with friends their own age and all other ages including Scott's mother- and father-in-law.

Life givers know that love is also persistent. Yet in many cases in offering help we find that those we offer help find it difficult to accept. Many times I have heard the words "I've tried before," "I'm too tired to try!" or "It won't do any good." These are the expressions of people who live in situations they feel to be hopeless. Hopelessness is perhaps the greatest enemy to life giving. People who have reached this state find it difficult to have faith. They are burdened with unresolved conflicts and unexpressed emotions. When someone offers to help and tries to enlist their own help, these people just don't seem up to it. This is one of the reasons why life givers must stay in the business of giving life. Some people who appear to be helpers and givers of life are really unloading their own emotions upon people who are already overloaded emotionally. Spotting such persons is fairly easy since they will take hours of time telling you how they feel or discussing their own anxiety. It is appropriate for a life giver to illustrate crises he has experienced or shared with other people. These serve as illustrations that something can be done but, such sharing does not require more than a few minutes.

A life giver like anyone who shares private information regarding others should always work to keep confidences which have been shared with him and to keep anonymous people and their problems.

Life giving love is never careful and as long as there are perishing people, life givers must not be careful. Lois Cheney speaks of this in her book *God Is No Fool.*

> There are those who reach out and touch us in their need. There is the God who opens us to another's needs, and this fits the crisis of Christian responsibility. We perceive it; we waken to it; and we yearn to fulfil it. The danger of the blunder, the misstep is as close as the glow of fulfilment. When the moment arrives, we must act in deep, yearning prayer. It is at these moments when God works most surely through us. It is so frightening that many turn away, afraid of the slash on soul and ego. For those who do not turn away, God blesses, promising nothing, but hoping deeply as we hope.[1]

NOTES

1. Lois A. Cheney, *God Is No Fool* (Nashville: Abingdon Press, 1969), p. 110.

NINE

Give and Live

I was standing in front of a rack at a community book store. A young woman walked in, asked the sales person if he had a book on palm reading. They began to discuss the subject. I easily overheard the conversation. A woman, who supposedly could read palms, concluded from reading the young woman's palm that she was going to have a tragedy in her family. Obviously the woman was concerned. She did not believe in the powers of the palmist but she couldn't get the irritating thought out of her mind. It had finally driven her to the only source of help she knew. A book store. Books are written by people to people therefore may give help. But this person needed a real person who could share and relieve fear.

On a recent air flight I sat by four different people. Three of the four told me of themselves. Each had a worrisome conflict with significant people in their life. One had three conflicts. Another had two. I have heard from two by correspondence since then. But these people need a life giver whom they can see, touch, and be with; someone who will find and stay with them until they have solved these problems. Who will it be?

Could it be you? Are you involved with helping people? If so, do you need to become a more effective life giver? If not, is it time you accepted this challenge to deliberately intervene in behalf of others?

This is an invitation for you to give and live. There are words that describe how a life giver feels because of his work. He thrills. He hopes. He lives. In giving insight he gets excitement. In giving hope he gets hope. In giving life he gains his life. Herein is the essence of the saying, "He who will lose his life shall save it." This invitation to life giving is an invitation to become a part of the movement of God's Spirit upon the face of today's world. The tides of evil move relentlessly upon all people. Surely we all shall perish unless some of us act courageously to stem this tide.

"But how do I go about it?" many people ask. The answer is in using your inner resources and a workable method. If you are new at life giving, try the following.

Get to know yourself and thus your inner resources. Think through your life from birth till now. Remember especially the events with which you associate strong feelings, good or bad. Recall the years of three, four, and five. Many people say they can't do this. Just relax and try. When you recall strong feelings decide what they are, why you had them, and who or what may have caused them. If they are negative feelings of anger or fear, deal with them as suggested by illustrations in this book. Catalog your experiences both good and bad. These are places you have learned. These are places where you should be able to help others. Remember you don't have to solve other people's problems. They need someone to understand, to offer insight, and to stand by.

Accept your humanity. Only God is perfect. It is in our human experience that we are able to gain insight that another person can use. By denying our humanity and cloaking ourselves with a false godliness we put a wall between ourselves and people who need help. We also hide experiences that can be stepping stones to life for others. Open yourself to the full range of human thinking, feeling, and acting.

Let God be God! He is you know! He will be responsible to do his work. Pray in thoughtful communication with God, but do your part in serving as an instrument of deliberate intervention and life giving.

See your world. This isn't your father or grandfather's world. It is the 70's world. Old answers may not work. Think what today's people are saying by their words and actions. Take time, certainly more than minutes, to listen and understand what the people you are trying to help are saying. Say back to them what you understand. Ask if you have understood.

Accept others as human beings; nothing more. Don't be surprised if they use language and describe behavior that is human; perhaps even common or vulgar compared to your own life style. On the other hand, they may be frightened persons that need you to say what they are thinking, feeling, and doing. Try it. They will probably tell you if you are wrong. Remember that if they were not human they wouldn't have human problems. Don't be fooled by nice clothes, gracious manners, or sophisticated behavior. Many people with such are masking the scars and open sores of unbelievable evil that they or others have perpetrated upon them.

Choose your own style of life giving. A woman engaged in life giving related to the western American Indian was describing lobbying activities she did. When I asked why she did that instead of several other possible things she replied, "That's my style." Every life giver should know his style and then improve upon it. Also, he should add new ways in order to be more effective. Is it comfort with a card or visit? Is it affection with perfume and a hug? Is it making cartoons that have special meaning to some people? Or is it listening, asking, crying, and praying with someone?

Practice makes perfect someone said. I doubt it when it comes to life giving, but practice will make your method or style better. So practice. Get a life giving partner who can let you practice on him or her. Ask for suggestions to improve. Try your style for real.

Intervene with courage and hope. Don't practice too long and don't wait. The world can't. Now is a good time to start. The people around you are hurting. Intervening is a result of decision making. Decide to whom you will offer help. Decide when you will offer help. Keep both decisions.

Know—Accept Yourself
Know—Accept Another
Choose—Practice Method
Intervene Deliberately

It is late at night in the waiting room of a large airport. I am watching a twelve-month-old child. She is full of energy despite the late hour. Everyone around is interested in her antics. Smiles and chuckles are on the faces of old and young. Tired faces have momentarily relaxed. She is giving life. Oops! She falls. Listen to her cry. See the tears run down her cheeks. Everyone around is anxious. Tiredness returns to the faces. Jeanette is on her way in life. Many times she'll have bumps, bruises, and breaks. Some will be physical, some mental, and all will be emotional. Who will care for her through these years? When she is old, what kind of story will she tell of her life? The answer is the same as that of an old story.

A Chinese youth knew a man whom all the community respected for his wisdom and helpfulness. The youth despised this man and in enmity set out to destroy his reputation and usefulness by making a fool of him. He chose a plan to do this damage. The youth caught a bird alive. He went to the home of the wise old man and called him to the window where the youth spoke to him.

Holding the live bird with both his hands, he asked, "What do I have, O sage?"

"A bird," came a quick reply.

"Dead or alive?" asked the youth, knowing if the sage answered "alive" he would crush the bird to death. But if the answer was "dead," he would release the bird to fly away to freedom and life.

"As you will it!" came the wise and speedy response.

So with Jeanette and millions more like her, it is as you and all other life givers will it. These unbelievable life givers have an unbelievable task they share and share they do.

The fellowship of life givers is not a formal organization with formal membership, but wherever I go I meet them. We share our successes and our failures. We pray together. We hope together. We look for new life givers together. We call to you to join us. And so with another life giver I call to you!

"To be loved is life.
To give love is to give life.
Together we live!"